PLAYING THE KEYBOARD IN WORSHIP

Copyright Details

Playing the Keyboard in Worship

STUART TOWNEND

KINGSWAY PUBLICATIONS
EASTBOURNE

ISBN 0 85476 288 4

The songs referred to in this book can be
found in their entirety in *Songs of Fellowship*
Music Edition (ISBN 0 86065 935 6).

Copyright holders and addresses are
listed on page 2.

Produced by Bookprint Creative Services
P.O. Box 827, BN23 6NX, England for
KINGSWAY PUBLICATIONS LTD
Lottbridge Drove, Eastbourne, E. Sussex BN23 6NT.
Printed in Great Britain

Contents

Foreword by David Fellingham 7
Introduction 9
   Why a book about keyboards? 9
   Training, not ability 10
   How to use this book 10
   Understanding music in worship 12
   Am I qualified? 13
   Worshipping and leading in worship 14
Chapter 1—Basic Techniques 17
   Dots or chords? 17
   Using the songbook 19
   Establishing and maintaining a steady pace 23
   Basic techniques for left and right hand 27
Chapter 2—Understanding Chords 30
   Chords and inversions 30
   More complex chords 35
   Chord progressions 39
   Related chords 42
Chapter 3—Developing Flexibility 46
   Learning songs by heart 47
   Intros, outros and turn-rounds 49
   Transposing 55
   Linking songs 56
Chapter 4—Expression and Interpretation 63
   Dynamics 63
   Changing key within a song 67
   Changing speed within a song 68
   Expanding and substituting chords 69
   Expressive introductions 72
   Instrumental passages 72
   Not playing! 73

Harmonising and counter-melodies   74
Chapter 5—The Deep End: Improvised Playing and the Prophetic   76
Improvisation   76
What is prophetic playing?   82
Accompanying singing in the Spirit   83
Accompanying a Scripture reading   84
Accompanying a prophetic song or sung Scripture   85
Playing an instrumental passage   86
Preparing for the improvised   86
Playing songs with prophetic insight   86
Chapter 6—Playing by Ear   88
Playing by sight and playing by ear   88
The process of playing by ear   89
Playing melodies by ear—recognising intervals   90
Playing chords by ear   92
Further tips   96
Chapter 7—Contemporary Styles   98
Elements of the contemporary sound   99
'Gospel' styles of playing   105
Latin rhythms   107
Swing rhythms   109
Chapter 8—The World of Synthesisers   111
Look—no strings!   112
Synthesisers in worship   113
Some practical ideas on synthesiser playing   113
The wonderful world...of MIDI   116
The keyboard action   117
Purchasing keyboard equipment   117
Appendix 1—Playing with Others   119
Appendix 2—Chord Reference Section   121
Glossary   123

Foreword

In the history of the church, styles of musical accompaniment for worship have caused much debate. The great J.S. Bach would often find himself in trouble with church officials because his music was alleged to be too ornate and inappropriate for worship. Churchgoers often have strong opinions on the subject, with the result that church musicians have to contend with those strong views in addition to their own desire for artistic and technical excellence and their desire to serve God in music.

The debate continues today with the rise of the contemporary praise and worship phenomenon. A plethora of new songs, albums and songbooks has revolutionised many churches, from the traditional denominations to the new charismatic groups. Traditional methods of musical accompaniment are being challenged by new songs which require different skills from the organist who reads four-part harmony from a hymnbook.

To accompany modern worship songs effectively requires a different approach to keyboard playing. There are many factors which a traditional four-part-harmony player would not have to consider. There are more keyboard instruments to choose from, and in many churches the pipe organ has given way to such instruments as electric pianos and synthesisers, not to mention such mysterious things as sound modules and MIDI.

The contemporary praise and worship scene which has emerged through the charismatic movement is more of a spiritual phenomenon than a cultural one.

As churches have become 'renewed in the Spirit' their worship has changed, often with a freer expression and more contribution and participation from the congregation. The accompanist therefore not only requires technical skills, but also spiritual sensitivity. Both are vital if worship is to be accompanied effectively.

The modern worship keyboard player needs an understanding of a broad range of musical styles. The playing and singing of hymns is still an important part of worship, but many worship songs reflect differing styles of music, eg:

The Feast	Graham Kendrick	Latin
There is power in the name of Jesus	Noel Richards	Rock
God of glory	David Fellingham	Slow ballad

Often the keyboard player has to work with other musicians, and rather than incorporating melody, bass line, harmony and whatever embellishments can be thought up, there has to be a greater sensitivity to how musicians work together.

Then there is the relationship with the worship leader, and sensitivity to how a meeting is being led.

The keyboard player may be asked to play sensitively during Bible readings, or to provide the right ambience when a worship leader is introducing a song or ministering in some way.

In the light of all this, it is surely fair to say that the modern worship keyboard player must be anointed, skilled, sensitive to the Spirit, and courageous.

I have had the pleasure over the last seven years of working with Stuart. He is a fine all-round musician with an excellent knowledge of Christian music from several streams. He is the most qualified person I know to write and teach on this subject, particularly because he has made these principles work. There have been many meetings where I have been leading worship and Stuart's sensitivity and skill have helped the congregation in moments of high exuberant praise, as well as times of gentle adoration of Jesus.

I believe this book will provide a much needed manual of teaching, equipping keyboard players to be more effective in serving the Lord in these exciting days where righteousness and praise are springing up before all nations.

David Fellingham

Introduction

Why a book about keyboards?

The keyboard has been the central feature of church music for hundreds of years, mainly in the form of the church organ. For centuries keyboard players have played wonderful music, written by the masters, everywhere from the humblest village church to the most magnificent cathedral. Given such a wonderful heritage, do we really need a manual on the subject?

If you play regularly at your church, you will not have failed to notice a significant change in some of the music you are required to play today. Names like Graham Kendrick, Dave Bilbrough, Dave Fellingham and Noel Richards now sit alongside Isaac Watts and Charles Wesley on our music stand, and they bring with them some fresh challenges to our playing ability. In addition, the renewal God has been bringing to our churches has often included a spontaneous element to our worship, requiring a level of creativity and flexibility not needed before.

For those of us with a classical training the challenge may seem too great. Accustomed to a more traditional style of music for which we feel trained, we are confronted with contemporary rhythms, melodies and chord progressions unfamiliar to us—and we feel inadequate. Perhaps some of us react negatively, criticising the songs (and the person who introduced them) and wanting to have nothing to do with this style of worship; it seems disordered, disrespectful, somehow out of control. Others of us may recognise the significant contribution these songs are making to our church life, but still struggle to master styles of music we have never played before.

Then there are those of us who are self-taught; our ability to read music may be severely limited or even non-existent, but we have trained ourselves to read the guitar chords above the stave, and we can to some extent play by ear. Yet we feel we lack the framework, the basic understanding of why things work the way they do. And we may also feel very limited in what we can do: we have developed a certain style of playing, but we can't break out into other styles and techniques, because we don't know how they work. We too need some training in order to make us more versatile and flexible.

If any of this describes you, then it is with you in mind that this book has been written. I hope that people of all backgrounds and playing styles will find something of use in these pages. Some chapters are geared more to some backgrounds than others: the chapter on chords, for example, may come as a revelation to classically-trained players, whereas the 'contemporary styles' chapter may be of particular help to the self-taught player who needs some pointers on how to develop a range of playing styles. I find again and again that it is the more contemporary music element in praise and worship, and the need for some spontaneity and inspiration, that plagues the playing lives of worship keyboard players.

Training, not ability

For the vast majority of us, the root of the problem is training, not ability. Although we may feel that we are simply biologically incapable of playing *Jesus, we celebrate Your victory* without it sounding like a pub singalong, it is simply because we are unfamiliar with playing that style of music. My classical training on piano never taught me to play in a contemporary way; I learned it by sneaking my book of Beatles songs onto the music stand during piano practice at home. And because it was pop music I listened to, which surrounded me in my youth, inevitably I began to try to bring it into my piano playing. If we were brought up in a previous generation, perhaps that of Bill Haley or Elvis Presley, then we may find that music more familiar. The big band sound, jazz, Jim Reeves, or an upbringing on classical music will all have their influence on us. We are all to some extent children of our generation and culture.

I hope that this book will give you some insight into the styles of music which feature strongly in today's praise and worship. Chords, rhythms and syncopation are all elements that can be grasped through training and familiarity. In addition, some pointers in the whole realm of improvised playing, prophetic music and sung Scripture will be included, to enable us to begin to step out in these very exciting areas.

How to use this book

This book has been structured as a progression. From the basic elements of playing in worship, we go on to learning to be more flexible, and then to learning to play with more expression. Then we shall enter the world of improvised and prophetic playing and the 'mystery' of playing by ear. I've also included a chapter specifically on some contemporary styles, as well as a section on synthesisers.

Don't give up your day job

It needs to be said that simply reading this book will not turn you into a maestro keyboard player overnight! The ideas set out here require practice and familiarity, and this book is little more than a catalyst for you to experiment for yourself and develop your own style—most of the work needs to be done by you. Equally, don't be put off by complex concepts. Often the explaining of an idea is far more longwinded than the idea itself! I have often found that, particularly in the areas of the selection of chords and playing by ear, the penny will suddenly drop for someone after weeks of confusion and effort. Although music is in essence logical, almost mathematical in theory, I find I reach a point where the fingers become so familiar with shapes and progressions I don't have to think too hard about numbers and letters!

This book is also not a book for absolute beginners on the keyboard. There are plenty of good manuals (and teachers) to teach the basics of hand positions, fingering, the names of notes, and so on, to start off a complete novice, and these basic elements clearly need to be grasped before beginning to play in church worship. However, the ability to read music, although helpful, is not essential, either to understand this book or to play in worship. Some of the most competent and creative worship keyboard players I have ever heard don't read a note of music. Although some musical notation has had to be included where necessary, 'non-readers' should be able to follow the basic ideas outlined using the guitar chords written above the stave, and it may be worth getting a friend to play the music for you. You may also find it helpful to refer to Appendix 2, where the notes of the treble and bass clefs are written out for your reference.

A rhodes by any other name

Just a word on terminology. A glossary has been included at the back of the book explaining the musical terms used, but I have also tried to define terms as we go along. But from the start I should explain my use of the term 'keyboard'. In the book the term refers generally to piano, synthesiser or organ, whichever is appropriate to your situation. Although each of these instruments has a particular character of its own, most of the aspects of this book will apply to all keyboard instruments. The term 'songs' should also be understood to refer to songs *and* hymns.

Where the songs I refer to have been used in songbooks, I have given a reference number. 'SoF' refers to the *Songs of Fellowship* songbook, where most of the songs and hymns can be found.

Understanding music in worship

This book is unashamedly about the practical aspects of playing in church worship; the theology of worship is not covered, as others have done so infinitely better than I could. However, it is appropriate for us, before we begin, to grasp the role of music in our church worship, as very often confusion and fear seem to accompany the subject.

'It's too emotional'

This is a criticism often levelled at more modern songs (although some of the moving old hymns make me cry far more). We need to understand that emotion is not wrong, and that when people worshipped in Scripture they were usually emotional about it. However, the core of worship is not emotion, it is truth—even if that truth causes us to become emotional. Our worship times should always include strong scriptural content about who God is and what he has done, or they will become just so much froth. Equally, we should not seek to suppress or avoid emotion in our worship, as that is an important part of our honest expression of ourselves to God.

'It's too repetitive'

Sometimes those who shrink from expressing emotion in worship will criticise repetition of a song. The Bible warns us against *vain* repetition, but the repetition of a song or chorus will often enable us to grasp the depth and wonder of what is being sung, and help us more fully to make the words our own. This is why we as musicians need to learn to be flexible in our grasp of songs, so we are not 'thrown' by the spontaneous repetition of a section of a song.

'It's too manipulative'

Hand in hand with the wariness of emotion comes a fear that music may be used to manipulate a congregation into a certain mood, 'hyping' people into an unreal state. Although manipulation is possible, we need to resist the idea that music is somehow an insidious, sly method of influencing people. Music is a gift from God, and it is clear in Scripture that in both heaven and earth music is used as a glorious way of expressing worship to God.

Often in this book I will refer to achieving an effect or an atmosphere. This is intentional—it is part of the power of music to stir things within us. As worshippers and leaders in worship, the question we need to ask ourselves is whether this is the *appropriate* effect or atmosphere for this particular moment in our worship time; does it fit with the direction in which we feel the Spirit is leading us? If we are seeking to be led by God as we play, he will use our abilities to lead others into his presence, and we need have no fear that we are 'putting one over' on our congregation. And as we work at our talent, we will become increasingly effective in our worship leading.

Am I qualified?

Often the awesome responsibility of helping to lead our congregations in worship can feel quite daunting, and we may feel inadequate. Although there may be no official qualifications required to play in worship, there are a number of qualities I think are essential if we are to lead our congregations effectively:

Servanthood

We need to beware the damaging pride that can come with visible ministry; a preoccupation with looking good in people's eyes, and developing an unteachable spirit. If we are called to play in our churches, we are called first to serve God and please *him*, not other people; and secondly, we are called to serve our leaders, and submit to their authority.

Excellence

Having dealt with our pride, we are then free to be the best we can for the glory of God. God is not impressed with excellence for its own sake, but he is pleased when we give him the best that we have. If God has given us musical ability, we are called to develop it, so we can give it back to him in even greater measure (Lk 19:11–26). This will inevitably mean—yes, you guessed it—practice.

Security

As musicians, we often tend to be rather insecure about our abilities, either putting ourselves down all the time, or being very sensitive to any sort of criticism. We must beware of placing our identity too strongly in our role. If our identity is built on being the church's keyboard player, rather than on being a child of God, it may come as a devastating blow if and when God moves us on to other things.

Worshippers

John 4:23 tells us that God seeks worshippers, not worship. 'Man looks at the outward appearance, but the Lord looks at the heart' (1 Sam 16:7). If we worship God from our hearts, then he is pleased. Simply being a good musician without being a worshipper will not precipitate Spirit-led worship, and therefore our offering will be unacceptable to God. We cannot lead others into God's presence if we don't know how to get there ourselves!

Worshipping and leading in worship

Having said that, an important distinction needs to be made between worshipping and leading in worship. Musicians often feel guilty because they don't feel able to play and worship at the same time. The fact is, if you are helping to lead the worship by playing, you need your eyes and ears open to watch what is happening. Often when leading the worship band at my church, I have been totally frustrated to find I can't communicate with one of the musicians at a vital point in the worship because they have their eyes closed! Being lost in wonder, love and adoration is great for members of the congregation, but if you're involved in helping to lead the worship, you need to stay aware of what is going on around you.

Now, you can still worship as you are playing and leading—you just need to do it in a slightly different way. Remember, God looks upon the heart, not the externals, and if your attitude is one of wanting to worship him, he will delight in your worship anyway, even if you didn't feel that *you* got into it.

One thing that helps is to make sure you pray before you play. Tell God how you are feeling: 'Lord, you know I really need to concentrate on getting it right in the worship today, but I still want to worship you. Pour your Spirit out on me now, so that as I concentrate you will still be leading me.'

Another route to worshipping as you play involves having an attitude of worship twenty-four hours a day. Learn to worship in your heart as a daily activity, and you will find your spirit rising to worship even as you concentrate on playing.

It's terribly easy, when we're involved in the mechanics of leading a congregation in worship, to lose the freshness of coming into God's presence. Having a daily worshipping lifestyle is definitely going to help, with no worship leader to watch, no other musicians to work with, and no pressure to get things right! But I would also recommend setting aside certain Sundays if you can where someone else plays keyboards instead of you, leaving you free simply to sit in the congregation and worship with others. You may have to make a conscious effort to switch off from analysing everything from a musician's point of view, but it's worth it! Times spent just worshipping like this will not only refresh you spiritually, they will probably sharpen your ability to empathise with your congregation, and so lead them more effectively in the future.

Chapter 1

BASIC TECHNIQUES

You have been judged on the scales and found wanting.
Daniel 5:27

Dots or chords?

Like many folk, I was packed off to a piano teacher once a week as a child and teenager, where I learned the basics of reading music and piano technique, fingering, and so on, and was exposed to some of the great classical composers and their writings. However, each week I would come home, leave the satchel at the foot of the piano stool, and immerse myself, not in the music of Bach or Beethoven, but of Bob Dylan and David Bowie.

In fact, it was a book of Beatles songs that gradually revealed to me the mysterious relationship between the notes on the page and the guitar chords above them, long before I was taught any theory about chords. As the same chords kept popping up, so did the same few notes on the staves. It meant that, instead of having to read every note written, I could glance at the guitar chords and know what notes I should be using. It was a quick way of reading, and I could never understand why someone couldn't write the chords above a piece by Bach or Chopin—it would be so much quicker and easier to play. (In fact, in my teens I was often pulled up by my piano teacher for attempting to fake the chords of some of the classics when they looked too complicated to read!)

17

Which is better?

Today, the technique of chord reading is predominant in contemporary pop music. Although the writing out of stave music is not exactly unusual, and is still common for some solo instruments and classically-trained musicians, most drummers, bass players, guitarists and even keyboard players are quite happy with a list of chords. Why is this format for writing music so popular today?

Apart from the fact that many pop musicians can't read music anyway (!), it is true to say that a chord gives them the basic building blocks of a song, while allowing them to bring their own style, expression and creativity to the music. Since specific notes aren't written down, musicians make up their own notes and rhythms, based (sometimes loosely!) upon the given chords; and if a group of musicians are working together in this way, they can play off and adapt to one another's ideas and styles.

The following example shows how a typical chord chart might be written out. Although at first sight the note reader may find it a little strange, notice that apart from the absence of staves, it does resemble written music with bars and beats.

Jesus is King

Wendy Churchill

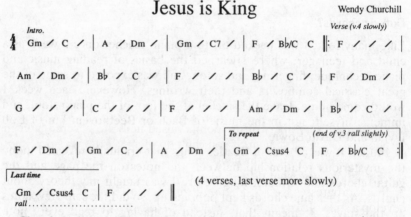

Chord reading does not do away with the desirability of being able to read music. To my mind, the two approaches complement each other, and are in no way conflicting. I find it tragic that the two are not taught together; classical training seems to turn its nose up at chordal knowledge, while chord readers tend to regard reading the dots as old-fashioned and 'square'. The first attitude stifles creativity, the second inhibits breadth and flexibility, since note reading allows you to emulate and enjoy someone else's ideas.

The ability to read music opens up a wealth of wonderful composi-

18

tions to the keyboard player, and is the only comprehensive written language by which musicians can communicate—it is an invaluable tool for the serious musician. However, reading chords enables players to stamp their own unique identity upon a piece of music, by individual use of rhythms and chord voicings; and attention to the chords helps them to appreciate better the musical structure of the song—how the chords relate to one another.

Now, while most of us will tend towards one camp or the other, it pays to have a foot in both. If your reading is weak, time devoted to brushing up (playing unfamiliar pieces, especially those without the chords written above) is time well spent. If your reading is non-existent, there are many good books on the market to get you started.

Equally, if your familiarity with chords is poor, then this is where you should start. As books on this subject are far more rare, the whole of Chapter 2 is devoted to basic chordal knowledge. Please note that this knowledge is essential if you want to move on to more creativity and flexibility in your playing.

Using the songbook

The first place most of us go to learn to play a song is the piano arrangement in the songbook. The standard of arranging in these songbooks varies somewhat (I speak as one who writes them!), but at least they should give you the melody, the words and the basic structure of the song. Let's look at an example of an arrangement, and how we can use it to its full potential.

Please note that many of the points raised here are covered later in this book, so don't lose heart if you can't do them yet! For example, not playing the tune in the right hand may at first leave you feeling a little out on a limb; just what do you play if you don't play the tune? But as the book progresses, you will find information and exercises that help to develop a style of accompanying that doesn't involve the tune. So simply treat the following points as a way of finding out what you need to work on, and then later you can use them as a checklist for learning new songs.

On page 20 you will see Dave Bilbrough's song, *Oh, the joy of Your forgiveness* (SoF 449). Now it can be tempting to launch into playing the arrangement, but it may be helpful to take things a little more steadily.

(a) Read through the words a couple of times so you really under-stand what the song is about. What moods or styles does it suggest to you? Where could you see it fitting in a worship time—a meeting

Slow 4

Dave Bilbrough

Oh, the joy of Your for - give - ness,
slow - ly sweep-ing o - ver me;
now in heart - felt ad - or - a - tion
this praise I'll _ bring to You my King,
I'll wor - ship You my Lord.

opener, an intimate love song for later in the meeting, a song that might open up a time for ministry?

In the case of this particular song, it is clearly not very up-tempo, but invites more gentle worship. As far as context is concerned, clearly people should be encouraged as they sing this song to receive God's forgiveness as a joy-giving experience, which could lead on to a more active expression of that joy in a subsequent song.

(b) Look at the guide word in the top left-hand corner to help you decide mood and tempo. Here, 'Slow 4' means just that—count four slowly! (The terminology also implies a slight gospel feel.)

(c) If you read music, play through the written arrangement a couple of times in the chosen style and tempo. The arrangement may suggest a style to you that might be helpful. I suggest you always sing the tune as you play. Not only does it help you to keep in mind the sentiments and meaning of the song, but it ensures that you play the song at a comfortable, singable speed.

In this song, the left hand is a steady bass line on beats one and three, with the added quaver fill. The right hand (apart from the tune) is playing a steady chord on each beat. This is quite a down-tempo, contemporary feel, further implying that slow gospel feel.

This feel is even further implied by the chord in bar four, where the D7 has an added F natural (this chord would technically be written D7♯9). Slightly discordant in nature, the note resolves in the following chord, but the effect is quite 'gospel'. The first chord should be emphasised by hitting it a *little* harder as a highlight of the song.

Also be on the lookout for distinctive rhythms. In bars seven and eight the same syncopation features in both hands. The second note each time is emphasised as shown, but beware losing your sense of timing as you move to the next bar. Try it slowly at first, counting the semiquavers to the end of the bar, so you don't cut the time short.

At this point, many of you might feel you have more or less learned the song: you've read the notes, worked out any difficult bits and decided upon a basic tempo and style. But if you want to become more flexible, expressive and creative in your playing of songs, you need to go a stage further.

(d) Once you are familiar with the tune, play through the song without playing the melody in the right hand (but keep singing it). You can either do this by reading the written notes, but missing out the top melody line; or preferably, if you can, read the guitar chords above the stave (dealt with in detail in the next chapter). Whether your chordal knowledge is basic or advanced, keep it as simple as possible—three notes in the right hand, one in the left, with no arpeggios or frills of any kind.

It might be a little difficult at first to play the chords and sing at the same time, without the melody present in the accompaniment. To begin with you could hum the tune rather than sing the words, so you're not having to concentrate on too many things at once. Start by playing it through very slowly, and only speed up as you feel more confident.

As you progress, don't forget to include the distinctive rhythms and features you discovered in point (c) above.

(e) Now look at the dynamics of the song—what are its high and low points; its loud and soft moments? Note that although the melody is a good indication of this, ie an ascending series of notes to a climax calls for a certain lift in the accompaniment, the central key to dynamic is really in the words. Read them through again, and look for points at which the congregation will be helped by dynamic playing. Let's look at an example from *Jesus, we enthrone you* (SoF 310):

The reason this line is repeated is not because the writer couldn't think of anything else to say! It reflects the idea of us building this throne for Jesus as we sing; stone upon stone, completing the way for Jesus to take his rightful place among us. We too need to build in our playing, to the climax of the last line, as we call out to the Lord.

Clearly it is important to understand how songs like this work. A line which makes a statement about God's majesty requires strength in the accompaniment, whereas words of tenderness may require a more soothing approach. The effect can easily be overdone, of course, and the song as a whole should not be varying dramatically in tone all the time. Subtle nuances, however, that help give shape to the song and reinforce the meaning of the words are vital to effective accompaniment.

(f) Work out an introduction to the song and write it at the top of the page. More on this later.

(g) After a couple more plays through, close the book and play the song from memory. This may be a little scary at first for some, but try it, and see how far you get. When you get stuck, go back and have another look at the song, then close the book and try again. Note that it is much easier to remember the couple of dozen chords of the song than it is to remember every written note. Chord reading will ultimately greatly expand your repertoire of songs from memory, as we shall see.

Establishing and maintaining a steady pace

Whether we read the written arrangements or use the chords, we need now to look at some areas of our playing style that may require work. And none more so than the area of playing at a steady pace.

Rhythm and speed are often problem areas for keyboard players. We shall look at rhythm in detail in Chapter 7, but regarding a steady speed, many of us have developed habits that are hard to break. Whereas in classical music speeding up and slowing down are generally regarded as legitimate forms of expression (in the right places of course), when it comes to leading a congregation in singing, a clear, steady pace is essential. It's even more vital if you're playing with other musicians! My experience of working with worship groups has shown up two recurring problems: the sound is too busy—ie too many notes are being played—and the speed is all over the place. Sadly, it's the keyboard player who's usually at fault, as they are most used to playing on their own, and consequently doing their own thing!

Here are some ideas that may help, and some areas to be aware of:

(a) When practising, play along to a metronome. Set the metronome (or drum machine if you have one) at an appropriate speed, and play through the song a couple of times—either reading the written arrangement, or reading the chords. Note where you tend to speed up—probably where the song naturally gets louder, where there are passing notes, or where there is syncopation. Concentrate on these particular sections, so you can achieve expression and dynamic without changing speed.

(b) Play simply. Try playing through a song using no passing notes whatsoever: just one chord in the right hand, and a bass note in the left, both held until the chord changes. Sing the tune at the same time, and hear how wonderful it is to give the melody a bit of space! Only then should you begin to add the occasional passing note—judiciously and sparingly. 'Frilly' playing, with arpeggios that sweep up and down the keyboard are not only rhythmically unsteady most of the time, they will excessively irritate the rest of your worship group, who find you've filled all the spaces they would play in.

So where are the 'judicious' places to use fills? As a general rule they should fit around the tune, not across it. Your playing will immediately sound too busy if it tries to compete with the melody—which is, after all, the central musical feature of the song. A melody needs to be given space to have its effect, and simple chordal accompaniment is usually all that is needed. As a melody line ends, it may be appropriate to use some passing notes to lead into the next line. Let's compare two examples:

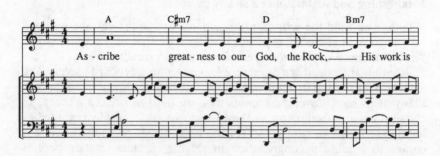

Here we see a flowing, arpeggio-driven arrangement not unlike many you might hear in church on a Sunday morning. It is not unpleasant, and it is definitely not wrong in any technical sense. The comment I would make about it, however, is that it's rather busy, distracting from the tune somewhat by its constant activity. Compare it with the example below:

24

Here the arrangement is simpler, still indicating rhythm and speed by the emphasis of certain beats, but remaining quite sparse when the melody itself is busy. Note also how the little fills (indicated by the brackets) become much more of a feature because they're not competing with anything—the song allows space for them.

Sometimes these fills in the appropriate places become quite important to the rhythm of the song, particularly if the last note of the melody is held on. You have to maintain the rhythmic pattern into the next section, and so prevent the congregation from coming in too early. Let's look at an example.

In *Amazing love* (SoF 398) confusion often comes from the long-held notes at the end of each line—particularly the first line. A small fill will keep the rhythm defined, and easily lead into the next line.

Note that the written arrangement uses a similar idea, in bar twelve, to link 'pays so dearly' to 'that I, the guilty one'.

(c) Check your introductions. Are they long and definite enough to give a clear lead to your congregation? They should be the same speed as the song itself, and not slow down just before the melody begins, as the rhythm is then lost. Hymns tend to be the exception to this rule, although many a rousing hymn has become a tedious dirge by a 'dragging' congregation put off by these pregnant pauses. For a change try maintaining a solid pace throughout the hymn. (Incidentally, if your congregation has a habit of lagging behind by half a second, don't wait for them, as you'll lose your own sense of rhythm.)

One technique I use for clear introductions is the loud-soft-loud technique. In *God of glory*, for example, we may use the last line of the song as the introduction, and as the line ends, gets softer, before becoming loud again just before the melody begins:

This may not be appropriate for every song, but in the right situation it will help to pull your congregation in on time. Note also that a strong vocal lead from the front, by a choir or solo singers, will help further. (More on introductions in Chapter 3.)

(d) Don't play the tune! It is often the greatest handicap to playing steadily and rhythmically, particularly when it's heavily syncopated and 'loose' in rhythm, as many contemporary melodies are. Often the rhythm of the melody is not the rhythm of the accompaniment, as we shall see later. Again it's worth noting that time spent becoming familiar with the contents of Chapter 2 will help you greatly in breaking away from the written arrangement and therefore having to play the tune. See 'Basic techniques' opposite for more help.

Not playing the tune may come as a revelation to some, freeing them to be far more creative with their accompaniment; it may be unthinkable to others. Whatever your feelings about it, if your church worship set-up includes a strong vocal lead or a solo instrument that can play the tune, or if the song is well-known, there simply isn't a need for the keyboard player to hammer out the tune. However, if this still sounds like musical heresy to you, one compromise is to play part or all of the first line, thus helping the congregation to get started; then they should manage on their own.

Basic techniques for left and right hand

Let us look at a few styles of accompaniment that might help you to break away from the written arrangements, if that's a problem for you. All the examples below are based on the chords for *Amazing love* (SoF 398). It's important to note that the melody of this song is very sparse and uncomplicated, made up as it is of long-held notes. This allows for a small measure of 'busyness' in the accompaniment, but please don't overdo it! Most songs we play have busier melodies, so our accompaniment would need to be simplified accordingly.

(a) Chords in the right hand, single bass notes in the left. Add the occasional passing note in the right.

(b) Arpeggios in the right hand, single bass notes in the left.

(c) Chords in the right hand, arpeggios in the left.

(d) A chordal figure or sequence in either hand.

(e) A combination of two or more of the above.

Although there are many other styles and combinations of styles that can be used, these three techniques are good examples of how to establish a strong rhythmic and harmonic foundation essential for leading the congregation. The basic parts when analysed are not that complicated, but even here practice is essential to make them rock steady (again, try using a metronome or drum machine to help you). We will look at these kinds of styles in Chapter 7, particularly the 'anchoring' role of the simple, steady bass line.

Note that the left-hand arpeggios, being lower, may not conflict so much with a melody line as a right-hand part in the same range as the tune; but too much movement low down in the left hand creates a dull, 'muddy' effect which lacks any real rhythmic or harmonic definition. Over-use of the sustain pedal will only make matters worse, so be simple and sparing!

In conclusion

Timing, sensitivity and controlled expression are the marks of a good keyboard player. It cannot be stressed too strongly that simple, steady, rhythmic playing is preferable to complicated, unsteady accompaniment. In my experience of working with worship keyboard players, I don't ever remember having to tell someone to play more. Almost without exception I have had to simplify the keyboard style. This is particularly the case where the keyboard plays with other instruments, and invariably leaves no space in the music for anyone else to feature. Sometimes simple, static chords are all that is required, leaving room for the acoustic guitar to take the rhythm, a solo instrument to take the melody, and other instruments to provide the harmonic interest.

Indeed, may I suggest that you adopt style (a) above for putting into practice the information you are going to learn in the next few chapters? It may seem excessively simple at first, but it is the ideal basis from which to explore chords and inversions, read chord charts, and develop your own unique playing style.

Chapter 2

UNDERSTANDING CHORDS

What I am commanding is not too difficult for you.
Deuteronomy 30:11

In this chapter we shall look at the basic theory behind chords, their inversions and voicings, and give some thought on how to fit them together into smooth musical progressions. If reading chords is a completely new concept to you, there will be much to study and practise here, but let me assure you that time spent exploring chords is time well spent—and it's essential if you want to learn to improvise.

It has always surprised me that, considering the amount of musical theory I was expected to take on board in my piano training, so little reference was made to chords and chord progressions—and yet for most creative players chords are the basic building blocks for improvisation and flexibility. However, if your background is similar to my own classical training, don't despise it; your familiarity with scales and keys is going to be tremendously helpful in understanding chords.

The following is by no means a comprehensive study of chords, but provides some of the basics from which you can begin to explore for yourself. It will also answer some of the questions worship keyboard players have often asked me about more complex chords.

Chords and inversions

Simple chords are made up of three notes—the first, the third and the fifth of the scale. For example, the chord of C major will look like this:

30

The second and third shapes are inversions—same notes, different order. Becoming familiar with inversions is important, because it will make your playing less jerky and more interesting. For example, C major to F major sounds better like this:

rather than this:

Why? Because we are playing both chords in the same range of the piano; the notes of the two chords are adjacent to one another—in fact, the middle C is shared by both. This principle of shared notes between chords becomes important when trying to link chords that don't fit side by side quite so naturally, as we shall see later on.

Bass notes

The simplest, and often most effective, form of chord playing involves the chord in the right hand, and a single bass note (or two notes in octave, shown in the bracket) in the left:

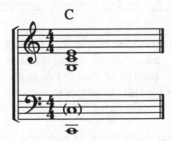

The bass note helps to emphasise what the chord is, ie C major, even if it was not clear in the right hand because of the inversion. 'Hold on a moment,' I hear you cry. 'Everyone knows that's a C major chord. You don't need the bass note to tell you.' Well, that's not actually true, as the examples below demonstrate. A different bass note can create a completely different chord, even though the chord in the right hand doesn't change, as you can see here:

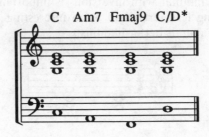

* This chord may be unfamiliar to some. C/D means the chord of C major, with the bass note of D. Similarly F/E♭ means a chord of F major, with a bass note of E♭, and so on.

Bass notes have a strong influence on the 'colour' of the chord, and can even affect the key of a song. Look at the example below, using the chord of C/D we just used above:

The progression begins in C major, but the C/D chord implies a new key to the ear; there's a kind of tension in it that is resolved by following it with the chord of D, but the D then needs to go to the chord of G, and we find ourselves in G major. (Note that such a technique may be very useful when it comes to changing key within a song, or between two songs.)

If you followed that, well done! If not, don't worry. The important point is that bass notes can strongly affect the feel or colour of the chord

32

they are played with. Try experimenting with different bass notes under a chord—either a note already contained in the chord, or a completely different note.

Notice also how clear the chords sound with three notes in the right hand, and just one in the left. As we noted in the last chapter, several notes played together in the left can create a 'muddy' sound, as the range is too low. Instead we have a rich, clear note in the bass, and the chord is played in the middle of the piano.

Try experimenting with where on the keyboard you play chords and bass notes. In the example at the bottom of p 31, playing the bracketed bass note instead of the note an octave below produces a gentler effect, while playing both is even stronger. Also, try using different inversions of the chord, or playing in a different octave. Note how a higher chord becomes less solid, with a thinner, more 'trebly' sound. In some situations, this effect will be more desirable.

So far we have seen the bass note as the 'root' or basic note of the chord, ie C in C major, or D in D major. Of course, the bass note could be one of the other notes of the chord. The effect can be interesting, but once again the unusual bass note tends to push the chord progression in a particular direction. For example, a D major chord with an F♯ bass note tends to lead our ear to a G major chord, as shown below:

Again, we see the bass note influencing the direction of the chord progression. In addition, the second example above demonstrates a basic principle of harmony writing which, although not essential all the time, is still worth noting. Whereas in the first example all the notes in the first chord move up to the notes in the second, in the second example the top note of A falls to a G, thereby contrasting nicely with the others. The effect, I think, is stronger, and is worth noting, particularly if a more classical effect is desired.

So far we have looked at simple chords and bass notes. It is worth noting that there are actually only four basic chords, upon which all other chords are based. They are:

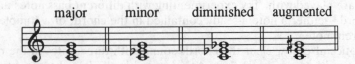

It doesn't look like many, does it? And the first two are by far the most common. However, remember that we need to become familiar with all the chords in all the keys, with all the inversions. That means learning the four chords in seven keys, with three inversions—a total of eighty-four. (And that's before we start experimenting with different bass notes!)

If the number of chords and inversions seems overwhelming, don't panic. It's amazing how quickly they become second nature, and you soon find your fingers naturally falling on inversions without having to think about them.

Diminished and augmented chords

We're all fairly familiar with the use of major and minor chords, but where do diminished and augmented ones fit in? They are not common in praise and worship songs, but as you begin to experiment and add your own chords to songs (see Chapter 4—Expression and Interpretation), you may find the diminished chord in particular very useful.

A diminished chord tends to move naturally to the adjacent minor chord, as you can see below:

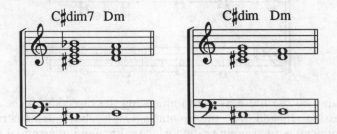

Diminished chords are often made stronger by the addition of the seventh note, as in the second example above. See how the notes slip so easily to the adjacent minor chord: it is very rare to see a diminished chord move anywhere else.

The augmented chord is even more rare, and is sometimes used as a rather old-fashioned way of linking to the major chord a fourth up:

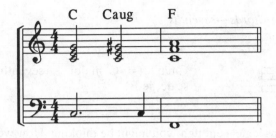

The progression at the top of the right hand of G to G♯ to A helps the transition from C major to F major.

More complex chords

For many of us, it is not the G majors and C majors, or even the D diminished or F augmenteds that cause beads of sweat to appear on the brow, but the increasingly common Gmaj7s, Dmaj9s, and the occasional A♭7♭9 (very rare!) that seem inaccessible. Where do all these notes come from, and do they matter?

It is important to realise that these chords are still based on the simple ones we've been looking at—in most cases we are just adding notes to them. The numbers actually relate to notes of the scale. Just as simple chords are based on notes one, three and five of the scale, so, for example, a 2 refers to the second note of the scale. C2 involves adding the note of D (the second note of the C major scale) to the notes of C, E and G.

The principle is fairly simple, but it has to be said that there are a number of exceptions, and these are outlined below. It would be nice to say that there was some simple logic to these exceptions, but unfortunately there isn't (without immersing ourselves in pages of complex theory that starts numbing the brain after a while). The best thing to do is simply remember them!

For simplicity's sake, all the chords in the following examples are based on C, although they obviously apply to all chords.

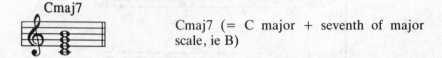

Cmaj7 (= C major + seventh of major scale, ie B)

That seems logical enough, you might be thinking. However, why is it called major seventh? We don't usually include the term 'major': the chord of D major, for example, is just written as 'D'. Well, it's because of the following example:

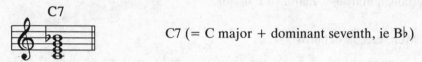

C7 (= C major + dominant seventh, ie B♭)

So 'C7' refers to something different from what we might have expected. In fact, C7 is short for C *dominant* seventh (sometimes written Cdom7), which is all to do with dominant chords in particular keys. Suffice to say that a C7 chord likes to move to an F major chord, thus:

This is classically called a resolution, where the B♭ seems inclined to fall to the adjacent A. However, for our purposes, we just need to note the distinction between C7 and Cmaj7. Another way of working it out is to play the 1st, 3rd and 5th of the chord, add another root note at the top of the chord, and then move that note down *one* semitone for the 'maj7', and *two* semitones for the '7', thus:

Cm7 (= C minor + seventh of minor scale, B♭)

'Hang on!' I hear you cry, the seventh note of C minor scale is B, not B♭. Well, that's not strictly true: it depends which minor scale you're playing. The key signature of C minor includes a B♭, and it's only that an accidental B natural is included at the last minute, so to speak, in some scales.

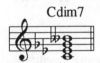

Cdim7 (= C diminished + diminished seventh, ie B double flat)

This completes the family of sevenths, where the diminished seventh is a semitone down from the minor seventh. (The note is called B double flat, but we know it better as A!)

Let's look at the four sevenths together, so we are clear on their differences:

Ninths and beyond

Cmaj9 (= C major + seventh of scale + ninth of scale, ie B and D)

The ninth is arrived at by counting up nine notes from the root note. It also picks up the seventh on the way, making a chord of five notes. It is the inclusion of the seventh that makes it different from a C2, which just contains a D, thus:

C2 (= C major + second of scale, ie D)

C9 (= C major + dominant seventh + ninth of scale, ie B♭ and D)

Note that the same principle operates as for sevenths. The minor ninth likewise:

Cmin9 (= C minor + minor seventh + ninth, ie B♭ and D)

Eleventh chords work in just the same way, only an eleventh (F in a C chord) picks up the seventh and the ninth on its way, making a six-note chord. Thirteenths add yet another note, and so on. But these higher numbers do tend to be rare in praise and worship songs.

It is worth noting that these more complex chords can begin to sound a little discordant, and it is the actual inversion you use that makes the chord work. For example, look at three ways of playing Cmaj9, below:

The first position, the root, has little to commend itself; it sounds rather awkward. The second is an inversion, but the effect of playing B, C, D and E next to one another makes for a very indistinct sound. In the third example, the muddiness is cleared by removing the C in the right

38

hand. It's still there in the left, so it is not missed. Using the bass note to avoid potential clashes is a trick worth remembering.

Suspended chords

Suspended chords differ from those above in that rather than adding to the three basic notes of the chord, they replace one of them—always the third note of the scale (the middle note in the root position).

 Csus2 (= notes C, D and G)

Note how this chord differs from C2, in that the E is not present in the chord.

 Csus4 (= notes C, F and G)

Traditionally, suspended chords are expected to resolve, ie it sounds like the F in Csus4 wants to become an E; and usually it does. However, increasingly you find that Csus*2* doesn't resolve—it remains suspended until it moves to another chord. (Look at all the suspended chords in *Glory* [SoF 128], for example, that don't resolve.)

Phew! That's the troublesome chords out of the way, more or less. I've included a list of chords in Appendix 2 at the back for reference. It's easy to feel overwhelmed by it all, but the theory behind it only makes it more complex. As you practise these chords in different keys, your fingers will become familiar with them, and they will add a lot of colour to your playing as you incorporate them into your style.

Chord progressions

Once you have a basic working knowledge of the notes involved in various chords, the next step is to string them together into a sequence. This is usually called a chord progression, and the idea of progression is important if your chord playing is going to work.

No matter what kind of music we play or listen to, there is some dynamic to a song or piece—a kind of building up or breaking down at various points, adding different 'colours' or moods to the music, taking us somewhere—and this element needs to be there in our chord playing if it is truly going to be a progression. We'll be looking at overall dynamic in a later chapter, but a basic prerequisite of being able to control the dynamic of a chord progression is being able to move smoothly from chord to chord. Awkward chord changes are a sign we're not really in control of our chord playing, and therefore we can't interpret the music effectively.

Here are some tips on how to effect smooth chord changes.

(a) Using shared notes. C major and F major chords both use the note of C, so why not play the same C in both?

(b) Using adjacent notes. The above example also demonstrates that notes next to one another work better than large leaps across the keyboard; the G moves to A, the E to F.

The above two principles can be used to ease potentially awkward chord changes of all kinds. One of the more unusual chord changes in popular praise and worship songs occurs in *God of glory* (SoF 137). 'You who reign' in line two involves a move from Gmaj7 to C♯7. At first sight, the two chords have nothing in common, and a discordant effect seems inevitable, but note that both chords actually share a B. Therefore, with the shared note acting as a kind of pivot, and the others falling onto adjacent notes, too much jarring can be avoided:

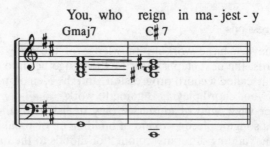

In fact, shared notes could be tied together, increasing the continuity

40

of sound. That is to say, in the above example the B in the right hand could be held on into the next bar instead of being repeated—it then really acts as a 'pivot' note around which the chord (and your hand) rotates.

(c) Using a short 'tune'. Sometimes chords simply don't fit well together, so a little creativity is needed. A short 'riff' or melody could be used to link the two chords, which gives the feeling of some kind of flow to the progression. In the above example of *God of glory*, one could play the following:

The riff, played here at the top of the chord, helps the link between the two chords even more. Another idea might be to use a short link of passing notes in the left hand:

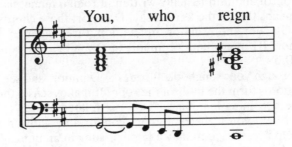

Practical exercise for chord progressions

Take the chords of a familiar song and write them out in the form of a chord chart, as we saw earlier. Play them through, chord in the right hand, one bass note in the left, all the time experimenting with inversions to avoid awkward jumps between chords; remember that adjacent notes and shared notes make for smooth chord progressions. Having found and become familiar with some new inversions, write out the chords again, this time in a more difficult key. This is simply done by transposing each chord up or down the required number of semitones; C major to A♭ major, for example, involves shifting all the chords down four semitones.

Having written it out, play it through, again looking for chord inversions that fit together comfortably, and keeping in a specific range of the keyboard. Make a mental note of new inversions, and practise them until your fingers are thoroughly familiar with where to go!

Related chords

So far we have looked at how we can link chords together, but some chords have a natural relation to one another anyway. This is more to do with the song itself and, more importantly, the key of the song.

The essential elements of a song are the words, the melody and the chords. Randomly-chosen words are meaningless, while a random tune is unsingable. In the same way, a random series of chords thrown together makes for a very strange song indeed! A writer tends to use chords that relate to one another within a particular key, and it is remarkable how the same group of chords pops up again and again in songs. This is obviously an advantage to us as musicians, for if we know the key of a song, we should be able to predict most of the chords that will appear.

In any given key, the three chords that are most closely related are the first, fourth and fifth (usually written in roman numerals: I, IV and V). This means that in the key of, say, D major, these chords would be D major, G major and A major. In addition, three other related chords are II minor, III minor and VI minor; in D major, this would be Em, F♯m and Bm.

Look through your songbook at songs in D major, and see how often these six chords form the basis of the song. It makes sense, therefore, to spend time becoming familiar with the six related chords of any given key; it will help you to become more comfortable with unusual keys, and will help if you have to play a familiar song in an unfamiliar key. It will also help when you come to improvising your own chord sequences. You may find it helpful to write out the six related chords in every key on a sheet of paper, thus:

	I	IV	V	VIm	IIm	IIIm
G major	G	C	D	Em	Am	Bm
A♭ major	A♭	D♭	E♭	Fm	B♭m	Cm
A major	A	D	E	F♯m	Bm	C♯m

etc.

42

(Note that this does not apply to minor keys, where for example IV would probably become IVm, and VIm might become VI. Minor key relations in the realm of praise and worship songs tend to be a little less predictable, if only because worship songs in minor keys are far less common.)

Before we leave the subject of related chords for the time being, we need to look at one useful link between chords that comes up again and again in the music we play. It is inherent in our western notions of harmony, and if we are aware of it, it can help us greatly in our chord progressions. It is called the 'circle of fifths'.

Circle of fifths

I promise to stay away from music theory as much as possible in this book, but this bit is quite useful! One of the strongest links between chords is when you step down five notes—a C major to an F major, for example. The other is when you step *up* five—C major to G major. In Anglican services, both are used as the chordal 'amen' response, and they give an air of finality and completeness to a sung piece of music.

These progressions dominate in the chord sequences of the songs we use, and the first of the two is almost always used to end a song. It is called a 'circle' because if you work through all the chords in one direction or the other—up five or down five—you go through all the twelve notes in an octave (including all sharps and flats), and finish up where you started. Let's look at the first of these two for a moment, stepping down five each time:

(This works with major *and* minor chords, of course.)

It is interesting to note that, if we think of each chord as a key, each change is a move to the key with one more flat, or one less sharp. For example, C major (no flats) to F major (one flat) to B♭ major (two flats) and so on. It is also worth pointing out that if we choose any one chord,

43

and we think of the next chord as the *key* we're about to go into, the chord we are on is the Vth of the new key. The move we make is a V to I move. This is how most of the songs in our songbook end, and it's very strong.

So how does this help you in your playing? Well, first of all, if you are creating an improvised chord sequence (and you will be later in the book!) and you get stuck, remembering this step-down of five notes may help you out. Secondly, you may have noticed already that this V to I move could help you get from one key to another, both to change key within a song, and to link two songs of different keys.

For the moment, don't worry too much about the implications, but practise your smooth chord progressions by linking chords a fifth apart, both with major and minor chords.

In conclusion

For some, the information in this chapter may be a little overwhelming. Complex chords with various inversions take time to discover and become comfortable with, but most of us tend towards particular chords we like and use them over and over again. With a little practice we can acquire sufficient chord knowledge to see us through. Others who are more familiar with chord playing will find a certain excitement in discovering new chords and chord shapes to enrich their playing, which will in turn spur them on to find more. Whatever stage you are at, it is the familiarity of related chords within a particular key, and the linking of these chords into an attractive, creative flowing style, which will mature your playing, and give you your own distinctiveness. You will then also be able to control the dynamic of the songs you play, adding emotion and power to your personal and corporate times of worship.

You may wish to try out the following exercise for yourself, in a key of your own choosing. Here I have chosen a relatively difficult key, B major, and have created a chord sequence using the six basic related chords as shown at top of following page.

Notice how the chords move fairly smoothly from one to another, without severe jumps. The next stage, however, is to add some simple passing notes that add melodic interest and dynamic, without the overall effect being too 'busy' (see second example on following page).

If you can begin to develop your own flowing style of fitting chords together, and even begin to invent your own chord sequences based around the six related chords, then you are well on the way to becoming a developed chord player and improviser. The principle of simplicity

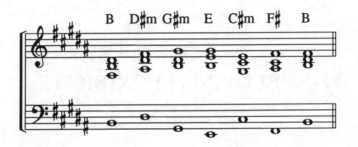

still applies, however, and a few well-chosen passing notes are far more effective than an unrelenting barrage of arpeggios throughout a song! We will look at style a little more closely later on, but at this stage the principle of chords as the musical foundation for songs is the essential element.

Chapter 3

DEVELOPING FLEXIBILITY

Let your hands be strong.
Zechariah 8:9

Perhaps the most challenging new aspect that the renewal of worship in our churches has brought, alongside the need to play a variety of styles, is the need to be flexible. You may play a song several times, repeat the chorus, or link it to another song. In spontaneous worship a song may be started by one of the congregation (inevitably in the wrong key and at the wrong speed!) and you are expected to join in. In some circumstances you may be called upon to accompany a spontaneous prophetic song, or a Scripture reading, or be encouraged to invent an impromptu chord sequence. Just learning to play the songs is only the beginning!

Although some of these events may often take you by surprise, you can prepare yourself somewhat by developing flexibility in your own approach. Instead of simply being a song accompanist, you can enrich the worship with your own creative ideas, and your ability to provide what is needed at the right moment.

You need to begin by realising that creativity need not be spontaneous. Some of what we look at in this chapter should be worked out beforehand, and with other musicians if you play in a worship group. If I am accompanying a prophetic song, for example, I am likely to use a chord sequence that I have used before, although it may need to be adapted. There is in fact a great deal that you can prepare for, even in the most 'spontaneous' times of worship.

46

Learning songs by heart

I am a strong believer in learning songs by heart. Freeing oneself completely from the songbooks may be too big a task to attempt immediately, but you can certainly begin to depend on your memory for more familiar songs. Many times in spontaneous worship the freshness of including an unplanned song has been marred because musicians are desperately flicking through songbooks for the right page when they should be playing. All too often the problem is confidence rather than memory space, and you can begin to develop your mental repertoire by closing your songbooks more often at home and playing from memory, as you were encouraged to do in Chapter 1.

But again, it needs to be stressed that playing from memory does not necessarily mean memorising the songbook arrangement note for note. It is far easier to learn the *chords* to the song, as there is less to learn, and it has the added effect of giving the song a kind of structure in your mind. Once this chord structure is familiar to you, you can even begin to play the series of chords in a different key, thereby transposing the whole song (more of this in Chapter 6). The whole song becomes more of a flexible instrument in your hands once you understand its chordal structure.

Let's set about learning to play a familiar song by heart. And they don't come much more familiar than *Shine, Jesus, shine* (SoF 362).

First of all, the chords in the form of a chord chart are on the following page.

Note that the tied quaver just before a chord indicates that the chord is anticipated, or 'pushed' (see Chapter 7, Contemporary Styles).

Now, play the song through a few times, working on using the right inversions to create smooth chord progressions. As you do this, think about the song's 'shape'—the progression from the intro, through the verse, to the chorus, and back to the intro again. Note where the song accompaniment feels like it rises and falls, and how that fits with the melody.

How will this help us memorise the song? Well, just as we remember melodies because of the shape and dynamic they have, so the chord progression has a shape and form to it that we can retain in our minds. We can begin to recognise intervals between chords as we listen to the effect they create.

Before you begin to play the chords without looking at the chart, examine them once more. Most of them are fairly familiar and predictable for the key—that is to say, they come from the 'family' of chords we looked at in Chapter 2. The G major, however, doesn't belong in that family of A major chords, and if you listen to it, you'll notice that it

A ╱ D/A ╱ | E/A ╱ D/A ╱ | A ╱ D/A ╱ | E/A ╱ D/A ╱ ‖ *Verse* A ╱ Asus4 ╱ |

A ╱ E/A ╱ | A ╱ Asus4 ╱ | A ╱ E/A ╱ | D ╱ E/D ╱ | C♯m ╱ F♯m ╱ | D ╱ E/D ╱ |

C♯m ╱ F♯m ╱ | G ╱ ╱ ╱ | Esus4 ╱ E ╱ | G ╱ ╱ ╱ | Esus4 ╱ E ╱ ‖

Chorus

A ╱ E/A A | D ╱ ╱ A/C♯ | Bm ╱ Bm/A ╱ | Esus4 E Esus4 E | A ╱ E/A A |

D ╱ ╱ A/C♯ | Bm ╱ Bm/A ╱ | G ╱ Esus4 E | A ╱ E/A A | D ╱ ╱ A/C♯ |

Bm ╱ Bm/A ╱ | Esus4 E Esus4 E | A ╱ E/A A | D ╱ ╱ A/C♯ | Bm ╱ E7 ╱ ⫶‖

doesn't sound like it does, either. It definitely changes the mood of the song at the two points it appears—building up a sense of anticipation, I think. Practise moving from the F♯ minor to the G in the verse, and the B minor to the Bm/A to G in the chorus, so that the sound of the chords becomes more fixed in your mind. Of all the chords, it is probably this one you are most likely to forget when playing the song from memory.

The song also uses a number of bass notes under different chords. Play the song through again, but this time emphasise the bass notes—you may find it useful to sing them at the same time. Becoming familiar with the progression of bass notes will help you to remember the song's chords.

Now try playing parts of the song without looking at the chord chart. If you get stuck, try to predict the next chord from the sound in your head—have a few stabs at getting the right chord before giving up and looking at the chart!

It is important, I feel, not to try to memorise the song by simply being able to recite the chord sequence, like one might a times-table, by rote. Training yourself to recognise the *sound* of chord progressions will be of enormous benefit, and we will develop this process in Chapter 6.

With a little perseverance you may find you can now play the chords from memory. If so, congratulations! If you did it by the process outlined above, you are well on the way to playing by ear!

If you didn't succeed, or at least found it very difficult, don't worry. You've still begun to turn what has been a primarily visual process of playing music into an aural one, and it will take time.

Intros, outros and turn-rounds

Part of learning to play a song is working out a way for the song to begin and end. Unlike the previous example of *Shine, Jesus, shine*, introductions are not usually included in a songbook arrangement, so one needs to be worked out. It may simply be the last line of the song, or the first line. Alternatively, you could create an appropriate chord sequence yourself. The important thing, as we saw in Chapter 1, is that the intro clearly indicates the key and speed of the song, and where the congregation is to begin (perhaps using the loud-soft-loud technique outlined).

When using the first or last line of the song as an introduction, you may need to insert a couple of chords, or an interesting phrase at the end of the line, to help link it to the beginning of the song. We saw in Chapter 2, with the loud-soft-loud technique, how two chords at the end of the intro of *God of glory* helped to give a clear lead to the start of the verse; just remaining on the D chord across two bars would have lacked dynamic and clarity. Again, the old V to I sequence helps here, as the most compelling way of linking to the tonic chord. But later in this chapter we'll look at some of the variations on V to I, when we examine changing key.

Outros, or ending the song, are usually a simpler affair, but exactly how a song ends in a continuous time of worship may well affect what happens next, so we do need to be aware of the effect we can create.

One effect is to slow down sharply, so that the song ends as a grand climax (see top of following page).

With the severe slow down, the congregation may respond with applause or exclamations of praise (if your congregation does that sort of thing!). The overall sense is of bringing the song to a fitting climax, and the music ends at that point.

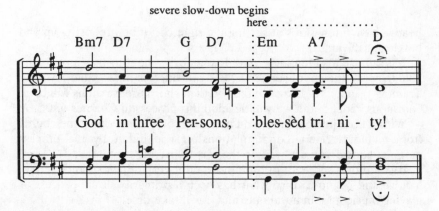

However, the music doesn't have to end at that point. It might be more appropriate to use the end of the song to link into something else. In this instance, a less severe slowing down may be preferable, when the ending is less grand and the music actually continues beyond the end of the song—perhaps to lead into another song, or singing in tongues, or quiet worship and meditation.

In many ways, this type of ending prompts more possibilities. Continuity of worship is often lacking in our services, and these simple links can provide just the right context for all kinds of expressions of worship. A musical backdrop for a Scripture reading, a prayer, prophecy or prophetic song, or simply for waiting in the presence of God; a way of moving into another song, or playing an improvised chord sequence, or an accompaniment for an interpretive dance—purely because you have provided the musical backdrop out of which these things can spring. Imagine how difficult it is to bring a spontaneous prophetic song out of total silence; a couple of gentle chords repeated a few times will make our prophetic singer much more confident. In fact, this willingness on the part of musicians to maintain a flow can actually help move a congregation into a whole new dimension of worship expression.

A third aspect of developing flexibility in a song is in working out the 'turn-round'; this involves linking the end of the song to the beginning again, if the song is to be sung more than once, or has more than one verse. This link will usually be straightforward, although, as with the introduction, a couple of linking chords may help (see later section on linking songs). Note also that the same loud-soft-loud technique may be useful to help bring the congregation in again.

But a turn-round to the beginning of the song may not be the only one needed. At some point you may only want to repeat the chorus, or the second half of the song, in which case a different turn-round will be required. This turn-round should signal to the congregation that you are returning to the chorus, perhaps by using different chords, or having a different dynamic feel. Look at the two examples below, using the song *Jesus, send more labourers* (SoF 300):

The first, leading back to the verse, becomes softer at the end of the chorus, and a slight crescendo before the first line of the verse helps to bring the congregation in. The second, however, does not drop down at all, but maintains its loudness throughout the turn-round, thus strongly indicating a return to the more strident chorus. And in this particular example I have changed the chords of the turn-round; the bass line in particular adding strength to the repeat chorus.

These techniques not only give fairly clear signals to the congregation, they add expression and emotion to the accompaniment, hopefully inspiring the congregation to sing with meaning. Try them out yourself, so you are familiar with how that kind of dynamic flow back to the chorus works.

It is worth noting that in order for a turn-round to the chorus to be played confidently, you really need to know that is what is going to happen several bars earlier—in other words, any signals from the worship leader need to come in plenty of time, certainly no later than the beginning of the last line. If you feel you're not being given enough notice, discuss this with your worship leader!

Repeating small sections

Repeating whole songs is quite a common occurrence in worship times, as is repeating a chorus. But sometimes it can be very effective to repeat a smaller section of the song, say the last line. It can help the congregation to focus on a single thought or phrase. In the above song, repeating 'send me, Lord, send me' once or twice rounds the song off really well, with the repeated cry to the Lord for him to use us.

How would such a repetition work musically? A convenient way is to change the last chord of the song; not only does it indicate to the congregation that something different is about to happen, it may also help you to link into the first chord of the repeated phrase more easily. The most common substitution would be to replace the last chord with its *relative minor* (worked out by counting down three semitones from the original).

Let's see how that works (see top of following page).

This link works well because the E7 to F♯m is strong, as is F♯m to A/E. Note how the descending bass line really makes sense of the progression, too, ending on the D.

This particular progression will work for a good many songs, because quite a lot of songs happen to have a IV chord beginning the last line, as above. Another example is *I lift my hands (I will serve no foreign god)* (see second example on following page).

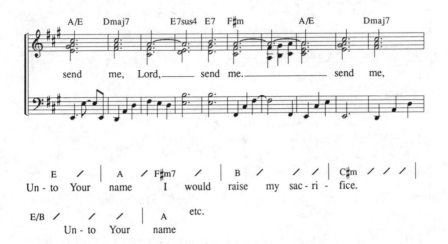

send me, Lord,_____ send me._____ send me,

E / | A / F#m7 / | B / / / | C#m / / / |
Un - to Your name I would raise my sac - ri - fice.

E/B / / / | A etc.
Un - to Your name

Of course, we don't have to use the relative minor, as we can see here in *Change my heart, O God* (SoF 58):

Cmaj7 / Em7 / | Dm7/ / / | G / / / | Fmaj7/ / / |
Change my heart, O God, may I be like You.

G / / / | Fmaj7 / / / | G / / / | Fmaj7 etc.
May I be like You. May I be like You.

Here we repeat the line 'may I be like You', but instead of using the relative minor, we go to the IV chord (here we're in C major, so the chord is F major). Again it makes a good 'coda' section, with plenty of room for louder and softer dynamic, solos, improvised songs, and so on.

Finally, let's look at the repetition of a line in the middle of a song. In *Jesus, Jesus (Holy and Anointed One)* (SoF 293), the song ends at the end of the repeated first section, but it can be very powerful to use the line 'Jesus, I love You, I love You' as a repeated phrase, before returning to the first section:

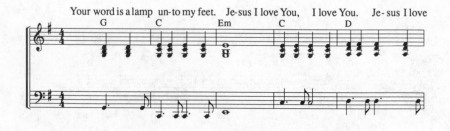

Here there is a definite build-up as the line is repeated, brought about by the ascending bass line, before the song drops down again on the last repeat.

It is important to understand that these techniques are not just clever musical ditties to prevent boredom in a worship time! They can bring a song to life by expressing its truth in a fresh, dynamic way. Of course, it's not appropriate to repeat the last line of every song like this; some just don't work, and some last lines aren't sufficiently strong in terms of content to merit that kind of treatment (remember Paul's words on *vain* repetition). It's only appropriate for the right song at the right moment; but when it is right, it can be quite special.

Try it out for yourself, repeating the last line of a song, and adjusting chords so that the link back works. The above ideas of relative minors and IV chords work for these songs, but really there are lots of other chords you can choose from, providing they fit with the tune and link back smoothly. Remember the tips for smooth chord progressions, including the idea of riffs and passing notes in either hand to smooth out a chord change. It can be great fun experimenting.

Intros, outros, turn-rounds and repetitions all need to be played with a degree of confidence. The congregation really needs leading at this point, since it is probably not sure what is going to happen next. Endings in particular can sound very messy if they are played hesitantly, and the result is an anticlimax rather than a fitting end to the song. Practise by yourself and with your music team to get the timings just right. It will usually help if someone is appointed to conduct the slow-down—the drummer, if you have one, or the keyboard player, or the guitarist. They don't actually need to fling their arms around in the classic sense of conducting, but everyone should watch them and listen to them. It's simplest to follow a drummer, because you can easily see his timing as he hits the drums. Keyboard players/guitarists may have to be a little more dramatic than usual in their movements in order to be followed. This person should also be responsible for count-ins to songs, so you all start together and at the right speed.

Transposing

The ability to play a song in any key is a tremendous advantage in a time of worship. For example, two songs may link together really well thematically, but be in different keys; if you can transpose the second song so that it's in the same key as the first, the link will be very smooth. (You need to check, of course, that the new key is appropriate to the second song; ie is it still singable?) Alternatively, a song may be started by a member of the congregation, but not in the written key. We have already seen that learning songs by heart need not involve memorising every note of the written arrangement, but rather by learning the sequence of chords. Then the song could be played in a different key by transposing each chord by the required interval—for example in a song written in A but sung in G, each chord needs to be brought down two semitones.

You'll probably find that this kind of spontaneous transposition *must* be based on the chords rather than the written arrangement—the ability to transpose a written piece of music instantly verges on genius in my opinion. I also have to say that it is actually quite difficult to transpose a song chord by chord in your head on the spur of the moment; it is very easy to get confused.

A better way is outlined in Chapter 6, where we actually examine the chord structure of songs. There we begin to learn songs as a series of chords related by their intervals to one another, irrespective of the key. However, transposing is a technique worth practising, particularly for when you are confronted with the music to an unfamiliar song that needs transposing.

The way to practise is simply to write out the chords of a song on a piece of paper as a chord chart, and then decide upon a new key to play it in. Here we've used *There is a Redeemer* (SoF 544) written in E major. Try playing the song in D major. Remember, each chord (and bass note) needs to come down two semitones. Play the song through slowly, giving you time to think as you sing and play. It's useful too to bear in

mind the chords you might expect to come across in that particular key
(see 'Related chords' in Chapter 2):

Verse

$\frac{4}{4}$ E ∕ B E | A ∕ E ∕ | F♯m E/G♯ A B | E ∕ B ∕ | E ∕ F♯m E/G♯ |

Chorus

A ∕ E/G♯ ∕ | F♯m7 ∕ B B7 | E ∕ A/B B ‖ E ∕ E/G♯ ∕ | A ∕ E ∕ | A ∕ ∕ B |

Last time

E ∕ B ∕ | E ∕ F♯m E/G♯ | A ∕ E/G♯ ∕ | F♯m7 ∕ B B7 | E ∕ A/B B ⫶ E ∕ ∕ ∕ ‖

Linking songs

Linking two or more songs together is an effective way of maintaining a
flow of worship, and avoids the kind of disjointed, stop-start worship
time that never really seems to get off the ground. In fact, a progression
of songs that fits together thematically and musically can be quite
powerful in helping to draw a congregation into worship.

Clearly, some songs are easier to link together than others. If they are
in the same key and of similar tempo, they should present few problems
(see, for example, SoF 281 *I will worship You, Lord*, and SoF 284
Jehovah Jireh as two songs that link very easily). Other songs, however,
may need some kind of link passage that will establish the second song's
key and/or tempo when it differs from the first.

Changing tempo

The general rule for a change of tempo between songs is to establish the
new tempo as early as possible, giving the congregation time to 'lock in'
to it. We can demonstrate this with *He is our peace* (SoF 166), going into
I believe in Jesus (SoF 203) (see following page).

The last line of *He is our peace* slows down a fraction, but on the last
word the new tempo is confidently set, introducing the new song and
establishing a stronger feel. This kind of thing does need practice,
particularly if playing with others, but it can work well. (In a worship

situation with a rhythm section, I would probably repeat bars 4 and 5 as indicated, to help further establish the 'feel'.)

An alternative would be to pause on the last word 'peace' for a few seconds, before striking up the new tempo. In some ways this is easier, as it gives you time to hear the new tempo in your head before you begin playing it; it also rounds the first song off more completely, if that is preferred. The important thing is to establish a new speed confidently and clearly—and if you do realise after a second or two that the tempo is wrong, you have a few seconds left to change it before the congregation comes in! (Incidentally, the way to remember the tempo of a song is to sing the melody in your head first.)

Changing key

Changing tempo is usually a fairly simple matter of establishing a new speed as early and as clearly as possible, but changing key requires a little more thinking and planning if it is to be effective.

The trick of inventing a musical passage to link two songs of different keys is to think in the new key and work backwards. In other words, if we are trying to arrive at the key of G major, we must find a chord or series of chords that naturally flows into G major.

So let's begin by looking at chords which lead into the root, or tonic, of the new key. Remember that these tips apply not only to linking songs, but to changing key within a song, as well as a guide for those 'fill in' chords you sometimes need to link an introduction or a turn-round to the beginning of the song. They all use the idea of the V to I cadence we have seen several times already. It's not the only link chord you could use, but it is far and away the most common, and is the strongest link to a tonic chord.

(a) V to I. This is the link at its most basic, moving straight to the V of the new key, and then to the tonic or root. In the key of G major the

cadence would be D to G. A further, more obvious (if more old-fashioned), variation would be D7 to G, where the seventh makes the second chord even more inevitable, as we saw when discussing dominant sevenths in Chapter 2.

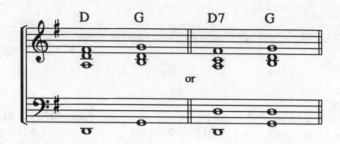

(b) Vsus4 to V to I. A further variation, just as strong as the above, but slightly more interesting. In G major the chords would run as follows: Dsus4 to D to G. That extra chord just helps establish the new key a little more forcefully.

(c) IV/V to V to I. Another perhaps slightly more contemporary sound, where the chord in the right hand moves over the static bass note in the left. In G major: C/D to D to G. This is really a more contemporary variation of (b) above (see first example on following page).

(d) IIm to V to I. A more subtle variation, which is often useful in more unusual key changes. This makes for an interesting but very clear establishing of the new key, as the chords flow so well together. In G major: Am7 to D to G (see second example on following page).

Notice that this exploits the 'circle of fifths' idea a little more, as each

interval is a fifth down (or a fourth up, depending on how you like to think of it). It makes for a very strong, smooth link.

So we have four strong ways of ending a link passage and beginning a new song. There are probably many more ways this can be done, but using the fifth as the final chord before the root figures in all the above examples, and is easily the strongest way of getting into the new song.

Filling out the first part of the link passage will depend more upon the key you are coming from, and as such is more difficult to create rules for. However, we have already seen how chords fit together better when they share notes, or at least use adjacent notes, and using this principle we can create effective and interesting link passages which maintain continuity of worship.

Let us look at an example of two songs of awkwardly different keys, and try our four methods of linking them. In our worship time we want to move from *Lord, You are so precious to me* (SoF 369) in A major, to *Father, we love You* (SoF 102) in C major. Using technique (b) the link would work like this:

59

The Gsus4 to G makes the new key fairly clear; the only slight awkwardness is between the chords of A and Gsus4; they share no common notes, and the effect is therefore a little clumsy. I have, however, tried to ease the awkwardness by adding a couple of passing notes in the right hand at the end of bar two.

Here we use technique (c), and the link is better, because of the note of A shared by the chords of A and F/G.

The third example below is based upon techniques (c) and (d), but with the added F#m7 chord to create more interest (see following page).

Here, F#m7 and Dm9 link together well, despite belonging to very different keys, by sharing two notes, the E and the A. The passing bass quavers in bar two further help the flow of chords, as do the notes in the right hand. The A to F#m7 is helped by the riff, and the Dm9 to F/G to G contains a little melody at the top of the right hand. The overall effect is smooth.

60

first loved me.   Fa-ther, we love You

One of the most difficult key changes is moving up a semitone. It is very difficult to make it sound smooth, as the two keys sound so different.

In a recording of *Crown Him with many crowns* (SoF 77), I had to move from D to E♭ for the third verse. I did it simply by repeating the last line instrumentally in the new key, thus:

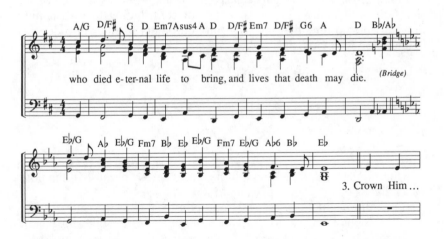

who died e-ter-nal life to bring, and lives that death may die. *(Bridge)*

3. Crown Him ...

Sometimes it is necessary to be bold rather than clever in our key changes. The important thing is for the new key to be established for the congregation. Note, however, that even here, help is given by a logical link of A to A♭ to G in the left hand, which helps the continuity of the link.

The possibilities of linking songs in different keys are endless, and allow a good deal of room for creativity. However, the link should be concise, as a long, drawn-out exploration of different keys may be enjoyable for you, but will tend to bore the congregation, or confuse them. I would also strongly suggest this kind of thing is planned and worked out before the service. Not only does it take nerves of steel and the brain of a computer to work out clever key changes on the spur of the moment, but it may also help the other musicians in your music group to know what chords they're supposed to be playing!

In conclusion

Flexibility is an increasingly necessary requirement in our worship times today, and if we think of intros, outros, turn-rounds and so on as a basic part of learning a song, we will find ourselves better equipped to cope with most eventualities. If you play with others, make sure you work these things out together, so you all know what is going on!

Linking songs can be particularly rewarding—not as an excuse to show off your ability, but as a means of contributing to a dynamic, flowing worship time that inspires you and others to enter into deeper communion with God.

Chapter 4

EXPRESSION AND INTERPRETATION

Do all interpret?
1 Corinthians 12:30

So far we have perhaps tended to be a little defensive in our approach to playing. We've talked about being 'better equipped to cope' and 'preparing ourselves' for surprises, almost as if a worship time is a battle to survive; an ordeal to endure with a minimum of mental scarring and confidence shattering! Hopefully, you don't view worship times like this. True, they can be a little scary when you don't know what's going to happen next, but flexibility and creative thinking can not only enrich your church worship, but be great fun as well!

The next two chapters deal more positively with ideas and techniques, some of which you may already be practising in your church, but others of which will act as a springboard from which to develop your own ideas, and those of your music group.

Dynamics

I have already mentioned how important dynamics are to almost every kind of music. Most of the songs you play have these sorts of dynamics, both musically and in terms of theme and content. Your playing should support the work of the song in drawing people into the worship and praise of God: gentle playing in expressions of intimacy, grandeur in declarations of majesty, strength in expressions of resolve and commitment, and so on.

Dynamic needs to be well-controlled, and not overstated. When you are playing a song, it's important for you to be able to hold yourself in check, so to speak, in the earlier part of the song, in order to have something in reserve for the latter part. Don't get to the limit of your loudness or forcefulness too early, and then have nowhere else to go for the rest of the song. The result will be that the accompaniment seems to lack dynamic, and gets a bit 'samey'.

If you can begin in a more low-key way, and only allow your accompaniment to become broader and bigger as the song develops in the minds and hearts of the congregation, then the song will be a more powerful and effective tool in worship.

You are probably familiar with using loudness and softness to accentuate different parts of a song. First of all, remember that getting louder doesn't necessarily involve being busier in your playing. You can easily get carried away and resort to the racing arpeggios and passing notes you thought you had tamed!

Individual chords or phrases can often be emphasised to great effect, by playing them a little louder. The best places to emphasise them are where the melody is held on one note, or absent altogether—that is to say, at the ends of lines in particular. The effect is that the melody holds centre stage, with your playing giving subtle and undistracting accompaniment. And as the line ends, the piano pops out with a little riff or emphasised chord before the next line begins. This is sensitive, dynamic keyboard playing:

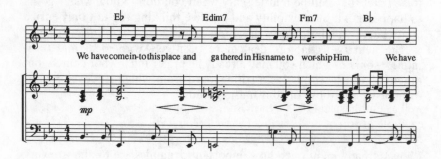

How you inject dynamic into your playing is very much a part of developing your own individual style, and ideas on dynamic and flow are covered at various points in this book, but it may be worth outlining a few extra ideas to help develop 'colour' in your playing:

(a) A quieter, more stately kind of sound, eg the 'quiet' verse of many hymns

This effect can be achieved by a more traditional four-part-harmony style of accompaniment. It doesn't have to include the tune, however, and it doesn't have to stick to four notes, or use the chords or the harmony arrangement of the songbook. Continuing with the example of *Crown Him with many crowns* from the last chapter, the quiet verse in E♭ could look like this:

This kind of accompaniment requires a slightly different approach stylistically from what we have been concentrating on so far, but note once again that even the greatest harmony writing is nothing more than a distraction if it obscures the tune—good writing works around, not across, the tune.

(b) Making the chorus of a song sound 'bigger'

There are several ways of doing this. One is to include octaves in the left hand rather than just single notes. This adds strength to the sound, as well as emphasising the bass rhythm, helping to lift the chorus, as in the example at top of next page—*He shall reign* (SoF 170).

Be careful, however, to co-ordinate with your bass player (if you play with one), as you have now well and truly entered their territory. You need to be playing the same notes, and essentially the same rhythm.

Octaves can also strengthen riffs in the right hand, and lift the excitement level. Passing notes in the turn-round of the same song sound much stronger in octaves than single notes (see second example on next page).

65

(c) Using different sounds

Organists will be aware of how changing the sound of your instrument has an effect on the dynamic of an accompaniment. Synthesisers, too, open up a whole range of textures that can be effective in a worship time.

Apart from the piano/rhodes option (see Chapter 8 on synthesisers), leaving synth-strings to play chords on their own to accompany the congregation makes for a very spacious, grand sound. Take for example this, from *Give thanks* (SoF 124) (see top of next page).

(d) Changing the range in which we play

It can work really well to move your accompaniment up an octave for one section of the song. It creates a gentler, lighter feel, which helps further to vary the sound of the song. The dangers in this are that a lot of movement in the higher register of the keyboard tends to be rather dominant and potentially a little piercing. Don't go up too high, and

make it sparse. The other problem is that it can leave a hole in the sound in the middle and lower parts of the keyboard where you were playing before. That really is the best range for the right-hand chords, so try to keep it more complete-sounding with the left hand.

Changing key within a song

We have already looked at ways of linking songs by a change of key, but a key change during a song can also add a great deal—particularly if the song is a long one. Normally one would move up in a key, as this helps to build the song to a greater climax; but it can also be very effective to bring a song down to a more meditative, intimate level by changing into a lower key. Whichever is more appropriate, the principles outlined in the last chapter for changing key work here too. Below are a couple of examples for *In my life, Lord* (SoF 242), the first moving up, the second down:

The only rule to bear in mind is that the new key must still be within the vocal range of the average congregation.

Congregations differ on what notes they can reach: churches in the habit of singing with 'gusto' can comfortably get a couple of notes higher than those who try to sing without opening their mouths! An average range is from the A below middle C (for a female voice) to the D just over an octave above it. Any higher or lower, and they may have trouble. Watch also if a congregation is being asked to sing a significant proportion of the song at either extreme of the range. A lot of top Ds, for example, will quickly wear down the enthusiasm of the liveliest congregation.

Changing speed within a song

Another means of providing variety in a long song is to sing a verse or chorus at a different tempo. Slowing down the final chorus causes a congregation to re-examine the words, and can shed new light on a familiar phrase or line that was previously glossed over. Note, for example, how the final chorus of *We declare Your majesty* (SoF 577), sung slowly, brings a freshness to phrases such as 'our God is mighty', and 'in adoration we bow before Your throne', leaving space for us to respond in worship more deeply than before. Sometimes returning to the original tempo once again evokes another kind of response; from a sense of awe, we can then be lifted up into joy and praise by a more vigorous tempo.

Simple tempo changes can bring a whole variety of nuances to an all-too-familiar song. As with all changes of tempo, it is important to establish the new speed as clearly as possible for the congregation. Use the linking chords between the last line and the section to be repeated to set the pace. Don't leave it too late; the congregation will need a few seconds to get used to the new speed before they begin singing.

Expanding and substituting chords

Chords can sometimes be made to sound richer by adding notes, based on the principle of 'more complex chords' in Chapter 2. For example, adding a major seventh note can bring a certain sweetness to a chord, perhaps most appropriate in a gentle worship song. It can be very rewarding to experiment with more complex chords, but it is important to use such effects only where they suit the song. Over-use can kill their effectiveness, particularly if they begin to crop up in every bar of every song; even great new discoveries can go stale prematurely.

Alternatively, an occasional chord could be substituted for one quite different. This can add interest to a particular verse, although once again the effect is spoiled if it is overused—its power lies in the fact that it is a break from the norm.

So how do you find a new chord that works? Well, first, it needs to fit with the melody, so preferably you should find a chord which includes the main melody note. Secondly, it needs to fit comfortably with the chord before and after it. Thirdly, it needs to sound right! In fact, the answer is to try it out. If it fits, and truly adds something to the song, then use it; if it doesn't (and be honest!), then throw it out. And if you play with other musicians, don't forget to agree on where and when to use it.

Let's look at an example. In *Holiness unto the Lord* (SoF 180), the song often ends with the chorus repeated several times. On one of these repeats, it might be effective to replace the Am7 in the second line

with an Fmaj7:

The chord fits the melody note and the chords before and after. In addition, it creates a stronger, grander effect than the much sweeter Am7, thus giving a different feel.

When exploring new chords over a melody note, don't be restricted in your thinking to simple chords. For example, if the melody note is a G, we know that the note of G is in G major, E minor and C major chords. But it is also in Am7, Fmaj9, B♭6, Fsus2, etc. That is not to say they will all work—most won't—but it is that kind of trial and error that leads to wonderful discoveries.

In some cases the melody over which the chord is sung will involve several notes. You need to make sure the chord will not clash with any of these notes, not just the first one. However, you can get away with passing notes which, if held, might clash with the new chord, but because the note is so short, it doesn't present a problem.

There are certain safe substitutions which you know will always work. Sometimes, substituting the chord of C with an Am7 will not be a problem, because there are so many shared notes. By the same argument, however, the effect is not as strong, simply because the chord sounds so similar to the original. If your new chord clashes with some of the notes, one alternative is to introduce an additional chord at the point where the clash occurs. But remember: chords need to flow easily from one to another, and a series of chords thrown together simply to fit the tune will sound contrived.

Other possibilities include using a 'pedal' bass note, where the chords change as written, but a single, unchanging bass note is played across several bars. In the final chorus of *For this purpose* (SoF 114), note how effective it is to maintain a D bass note over the first two lines of the chorus, moving them to a C♯ bass under the F♯ chord on 'sick-ness', as shown:

70

over sin He has con-quered, Halle-lu-jah, He has con-quered, over death vic-tor-ious, Hal-le-

lu jah, victorious. Over sickness He has triumphed, Halle-lu jah, He has triumphed. Je-sus reigns

Conversely, bass notes can be made to move under static chords, or, as in the example below from *O sacred head once wounded* (SoF 446), a completely new ascending bass line could operate under the chords:

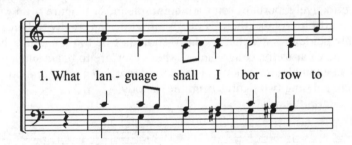

Adding chords

We don't necessarily have to substitute chords to be creative. We can also put an additional chord in between two existing ones, to put a new colour into the link. We have already discussed how a diminished seventh links in well to an adjacent minor chord, and here is an example of it working as an additional, 'colouring' chord in *Father, we love You* (SoF 102) (see top of next page).

But there are many other colourful chords we could add to a song. The same principles apply, however: a chord needs to link smoothly to the preceding and following chord, it shouldn't clash with the tune, and it shouldn't be overdone—*one* special chord *once* in a song is probably enough.

Glo - ri - fy Your name, Glo - ri - fy Your name,

Expressive introductions

We have already seen how the last line can be used as a clear, straight-forward intro for a song. However, you need not be restricted to this. You could create your own chord sequence which might introduce it more effectively, perhaps using a memorable musical figure from within the song itself. Again, there is plenty of scope for creativity here, and the only guidelines are that the intro shouldn't be too long, and that it should be clear to the congregation where they are to begin singing.

As an example, let us look at the song *I worship You, Almighty God* (SoF 282). Using two figures from the melody,

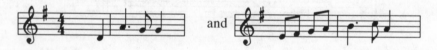

and

we can construct a creative intro that sets a mood of worship and reflection appropriate to the song (see top of following page).

Instrumental passages

Often it is appropriate for the musicians to play through a verse or chorus instrumentally. This gives space for quiet meditation and reflection by the congregation. This usually needs a word of explanation from the minister or worship leader, thus avoiding the expressions of bewilderment and embarrassment that can often be seen on people's faces when the instrumental section begins.

Another idea that often works, instead of playing through part of the

song, is to create a short instrumental section or 'bridge' of your own which, while being in keeping with the song, acts as a kind of brief interlude, and gives further opportunity for reflection, before clearly leading back into the song. Such devices, far from being self-indulgent, can significantly help a congregation to appreciate a song or particular truth in a new light, by giving room for consideration and reflection. It can also help to break up songs that have many verses. Here is an example:

We'll be covering how to create improvised passages in the next chapter, but in this context it is just worth noting that the passage above begins early enough for people to recognise it for what it is. If improvisation starts too late, or it sounds too similar to the usual turn-round, you may find people have already started singing the next verse.

Not playing

This may sound strange, but musicians can add as much to a verse, or even a whole song, by not playing as they can be playing. In fact, not playing actually heightens the effectiveness of what you *do* play. This is

73

supremely true for solo instruments, but it also applies in some measure to rhythm section instruments such as the keyboard. You may feel that the whole thing will fall apart if you stop playing, but dropping out of one section of a song and leaving the guitar to play alone, or even the voices to sing unaccompanied, can have a significant effect. Once again it should be stressed that leaving space for other instruments to feature makes for a far better sound.

Harmonising and counter-melodies

So far we have looked at playing creatively in rather sectional terms, but, of course, we can bring creativity to the very fabric of a song by use of harmonies, counter-melodies and so on.

For example, in the following song—*O, Lord, Your tenderness* (SoF 430)—a simple harmonising phrase in the right hand accompanies the sung melody, while the left hand provides the flowing movement:

Again, this device works best when used for one section of verse, never all the way through.

Counter-melodies or answer phrases fit around the melody, answering it in some way. Such a phrase may in some way resemble the melody in rhythm or tune, but there's nothing to say it should. Many songs don't leave any room between lines for an answer phrase to work, but one that does is *Jesus, Jesus, Jesus (Your love has melted my heart)* (SoF 294). It could be an exact echo of the melody, or a variation on it:

Here the answer phrase sustains the interest over the held melody note. Be careful that such a phrase does not clash with the melody itself at the beginning or end of the phrase, or the overall effect will be untidy. Also, be critical about whether it works. Don't try to squeeze in a phrase if there isn't really any room.

In conclusion

This chapter has presented just a few ideas on how to bring greater expression and creativity to your playing in worship. There are limitless possibilities beyond these, but the essence of all these devices is to interpret the song in the way you feel appropriate, thereby helping to bring out more meaning and impact in the songs you use.

When we are discussing the whole area of dynamic, it needs to be pointed out again that regular changes of pace are not helpful to a congregation's singing. The best rendition of a song to my ear is when the pianist and congregation are together, not when they are constantly trying to catch each other up. And when other musicians are involved, the need for a steady rhythm is even more essential. I believe we should be looking for other ways to bring expression to our playing, such as those outlined above. We can be expressive and steady in our rhythm at the same time.

Chapter 5

THE DEEP END: IMPROVISED PLAYING AND THE PROPHETIC

This is a profound mystery...
Ephesians 5:32

Despite what we have learned so far about chords and creative playing, the idea of improvisation will strike many of us with terror. No notes to read, no chords to follow, no defined melody; just a period of time in which we are expected to make something up—the whole idea seems horrendous! If you can identify with these feelings, I hope that this chapter, together with the following one which deals with playing by ear, will prove helpful.

If the world of improvising is a mystery, then the prophetic may seem completely baffling. Certainly there often appears to be an aura of mystique that surrounds the idea of prophecy, which keeps many of us at a (sometimes sceptical) distance. However, as with most spiritual gifts, the reality if far more down-to-earth than it might at first appear. We'll look at this whole area of the prophetic in a moment.

Improvisation

Improvisation is a huge subject, and we can only touch on a few points here. It is an area in which venturing out and being creative really does bring its rewards, and can be one of the most satisfying aspects of playing music. We all have a creative spark within us, since we are made in the image of the most creative Being of all, and I find it heartening to

76

see descriptions in the Bible of God using his musical ability as an example to us (eg, Ps 68:6; Zeph 3:17).

We have already seen in the previous chapter how we can improvise by substituting chords, and giving songs fresh treatments and styles. But when it comes to creating improvised passages of music, it's much closer to the process of songwriting itself.

A song is essentially a melody with words, supported by a series of chords. Aside from the lyrics, our ear is most interested by a melodic line, and the more appealing the line, the more we like the music. We can think of invented musical passages in the same way, and the place to begin is with finding a melody.

(a) Melodies

One way to find a tune is to sit by yourself and sing or play any lines that come into your head, until you find one you like. Consciously try to vary the notes and the rhythm, so that they remain interesting, and look for pleasant-sounding intervals between notes—fifths, fourths, thirds, octaves and so on. You may also find it helps to focus your thinking if you work from the notes of a particular scale, major or minor. Play it or sing it through before you begin. It will help you to home in on a limited number of notes which work together.

If you've never tried making up a melody before, you might be surprised (and impressed!) by what you come up with. If you can write music, you might want to jot it down (write down the key and time signatures otherwise you might be baffled when you come back to it). Alternatively, use a cassette recorder as a musical notepad.

If you have one or two phrases you'd like to work with, you're ready to move on to finding chords to accompany the melody. If you're still stuck, either because you are being too much of a perfectionist, or you really can't come up with anything, you could try this simple approach. One ex-music student tells me he couldn't be bothered to write his final piece of work for his composition exam, so the night before the deadline he took the music for a Bach fugue, turned it upside down on the music stand, and wrote it out. And he passed the exam with flying colours!

I'm not for one moment suggesting you should adopt this approach to composition. There's more to writing songs than copying out an inverted *Songs of Fellowship* book. But it might be a good starting point for some, a base from which to develop your own ideas. Take, for example, one line from the beautiful melody of *Dear Lord and Father of mankind* (SoF 79):

Let's invert it by reversing the order of the notes, while keeping the rhythm:

The melody takes on a new character, although I think some of the beauty of the original remains in the intervals between notes. Whereas the original was building to a climax with the ascending repeated phrase, now the effect is more gentle and thoughtful, but not without beauty.

Creating chord sequences for melodies

Once you've found a melody line you like, you need to fit chords to it. Once again your knowledge of related chords will help you here (see Chapter 2), but do not be restricted to those chords.

You may already find that your melody suggests some chords to you—you may not know what the chords are, but by trial and error you will be able to find them on the keyboard. If you get stuck at some point, you can resort to the technique discussed in Chapter 4 of working through all the chords that contain the melody note(s), until you find one that also fits with the previous and following chord. The 'circle of fifths' may also get you out of trouble, but at the same time be inventive in the chords (and bass notes) you use. This process really is all about trial and error.

If you don't know where to begin in finding chords to fit, simply assemble three or four from the family of chords in an order that sounds pleasing, and work from there, amending the melody as necessary.

Let's take a short phrase and fit some chords to it:

The most obvious chords that fit are:

But, by using relative minors, and a little imagination

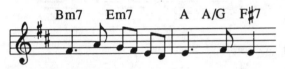

we find ourselves heading in a new direction for the next stage of the passage. Note how the passing note of G in the left hand helps smooth the link between the A and F♯ chords.

See also how chords which move in the same direction as the tune

can be made more interesting to the ear by moving the opposite way:

This is especially true of bass lines, which can provide an excellent contrast to the melody.

Once you have created a phrase, you then need to develop it by adding other phrases and chords. However, keep the whole passage quite short overall, as this helps to give it some form and shape. It is better to work with a repeated, interesting four-liner (or even two in some cases) than a long, meandering series of notes and chords—unless that is the specific effect required. Repetition also enables other musicians and singers to become familiar with what you're doing, and so join in.

Take care to vary the direction, range and rhythm of melodies between phrases, so that there is musical interest for the listener.

Continuity in improvised passages

It is possible to reuse the same musical idea in different ways within a passage; in fact, it really helps make for continuity. We have already seen this kind of idea in the phrase from *Dear Lord and Father*, where:

is repeated one note up.

As pointed out, the effect is of building up to a high point; the repetition is a powerful part of the process.

We can see the same idea below, where a phrase is repeated down a minor third:

The exact repetition of a phrase can also work if the chords beneath it are changed (see example at top of following page).

This actually allows for the chords to be quite elaborate or unusual, as it is the repetition of the melody that holds the piece together.

(b) Chords

Beginning with a melody is only one way of approaching an improvised passage. Alternatively, you could begin with a series of chords, and only add short pieces of melody or musical figures as suitable links between

the chords. This is more of an accompaniment-style passage, allowing room for other things to happen over the top of it: an improvised prophetic song, a Scripture reading, a solo from another instrument, or a spoken prophecy or prayer.

Here too the family of chords will prove useful once you have decided on a key, and once again keep the chord sequence quite short and repetitive if others are to join in with it musically.

Don't think that improvised chordal passages have to be intricate or clever to be effective. It has more to do with the texture of the sound and the mood and style of the playing than the originality of the notes. On the classical flute album *Here is love*, for example, the piano intro to *Great is the Lord* (SoF 145) is very subdued:

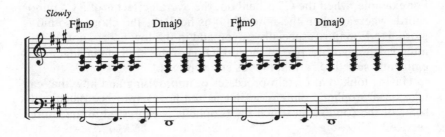

But the effect is spacious, and rather mysterious, introducing a sense of awe into the song at various points.

(c) Musical figures, or 'riffs'

Another approach to improvised passages is to take a repetitive figure which is maintained throughout the piece. It may just be a few notes, but it acts as what is often called the 'hook', upon which the rest of the passage hangs. Let's look at an example:

This theme could be played in the right hand all the way through the piece, with the left hand providing a kind of melody line:

Notice how the left-hand part, in addition to providing the interest of a melody, is giving an impression of chord changes, as it implies different root notes (the right-hand figure is rather ambiguous chordally). For example, when the C♯ is held on, the overall effect is of a C♯ minor chord, whereas when the note of G♯ is held on, the chordal sound is more like E major (especially as you add in the low E bass note). This intended ambiguity is part of the attraction of this kind of playing, and is eminently suited to certain moods and contexts.

Having looked at certain processes of improvising and how that can take on a prophetic dimension, let us see how improvisation fits into some of the contexts in which the prophetic is expressed in the church service.

What is prophetic playing?

As we meet together as a church, we find that God wants to speak to us about specific things. These things do not add to Scripture or lead us away from it; on the contrary, they take thoughts or pictures consistent with (and sometimes directly from) the Bible, and bring particular emphasis to them as the Holy Spirit leads. Often these pictures and ideas can be powerfully expressed with music, just as our praise is enhanced by musical accompaniment. Scriptures (spoken or sung), prophetic songs and prophetic statements with musical backing are all part of God bringing to our attention aspects of his character and revealed will.

Sometimes musicians are moved to improvise without words being used at all, simply playing expressive melodies and chords. Although this kind of prophetic playing is not as defined or specific as the spoken word, God still uses it to speak to us—just as music and art can articulate things on a deeper level than words can express. True, such playing is very much a subjective experience for the listener, and therefore a specific interpretation should be held somewhat lightly, but we must not ignore the fact that God uses such means to communicate his heart, and he is under no obligation whatsoever to limit his expression to the spoken word.

The Scriptures show instances of gifted musicians ministering to the Lord in music (eg, 1 Chron 9:33), and David's playing has a dramatic effect in the spiritual realm (1 Sam 16:23). God does not need words to convey his meaning or accomplish his purposes.

So how can we make ourselves available for God to speak through our music? Just as in any other area of our Christian lives, if we ask with humility and receive with faith, we will find that God begins to use our creative ideas, and even increase our natural abilities. Sometimes we will need to be bold, and risk looking silly, in order to develop a truly prophetic ministry.

Accompanying singing in the Spirit

As you finish a song, it may happen that people express their worship by singing together in an improvised way, or by singing in tongues. We saw in Chapter 3 how a less severe slowing down at the end of a song enables us to continue playing a chord, which provides a basic key in which people can sing.

As they sing, continue playing the chord, perhaps in a flowing arpeggio movement across the keyboard. The overall effect will probably begin in an abstract rhythm, but as time goes on, you might gently begin to inject a little rhythmic shape into it. Be aware of where you might get louder and softer as the singing increases and decreases in volume. Sometimes it is better for the congregation to follow your lead in varying the volume. Do not be afraid to lead them in this way. People often need encouragement to sing out like this, and it is part of your role to lead the people in worship.

There is no reason why you should be restricted to one chord. However, don't expect the congregation to change notes with you! It is better, therefore, to use a series of similar chords within the same key, so that the chords can move without people having to find new notes to sing.

The advantage of changing chords is that it can give some shape to the singing. A series of chords—say, for example, I to VIm7 to IVmaj7 to IV/V in any particular key (eg C to Am7 to Fmaj7 to F/G)—will not create any discordant clashes with the singing, and yet it might open up the way for someone to begin a prophetic song. These chords work because they all have a large number of shared notes—all based around the tonic chord. Try it for yourself in, say, C major. As you play each of the four chords, sing the scale of C major over it (unless your congregation is atonal or tone deaf, they are likely to be using only notes from that scale for their singing in the Spirit!), and you will see that all the chords fit comfortably underneath the scale. (Note that I've used a IV/V not a V, to round off the sequence. The V or dominant chord, although logical from a musical point of view, introduces a number of notes that potentially clash with some of the notes of the scale. In C major, for example, if some of the congregation are singing the note of E, the V chord of G will sound a little discordant, and may put people off a little.)

Other chord sequences will also work, of course. The simple test is to try them out at home and sing over them yourself, either the scale of the key you are in—or try singing in the Spirit!

Accompanying a Scripture reading

Coming out of a time of singing in the Spirit, someone may read out a passage from the Bible. Rather than stop playing at that point, it can be very effective to accompany it. Listen to the mood and content of the passage (if a Bible is handy, see if someone can find it for you and hold it for you to see), and try to set a generally appropriate mood—should it be major or minor, strong or gentle, loud or soft? Play a simple, repetitive chord sequence. Not only will this give form to the musical passage, but it will also help any other musicians who are with you to join in.

Playing with other musicians in this way can be quite exciting; a short musical theme or melody may develop which can be used and adapted by different instruments. Also, watch out for mood changes in the Bible passage which could be reflected in your accompaniment; a change from minor to major, a key change, or a change in rhythm could all help to give added impact to the words.

A couple of words of warning might be appropriate here. First of all, don't overdo it. Musicians can become so engrossed in their improvisation that they swamp the reading, and all that can be heard is a music group having an almighty jam session.

Secondly, beware of too literal an interpretation. Silent-movie-style accompaniments are inappropriate, as is the sound-effects approach, where every act of violence is accompanied by a diminished chord and a sickening crunch, and every reference to a king denotes a fanfare! A general mood is the most appropriate approach.

Accompanying a prophetic song or sung Scripture

Some people are particularly good at creating short improvised songs expressing what they feel God wants to say. These songs can be extraordinarily powerful, but they can also be the most difficult to accompany! They require some sensitivity on the part of the musician, whose job it is to support the singer in terms of key, dynamic and general song shape. Much depends on the ability of the singer, and it often takes a long time for singer and musician to develop a rapport.

The following pointers may be helpful:

(a) Keep your accompaniment simple at first, and let the singer lead.

(b) Does the sung passage have a song-like shape—lines of similar length, perhaps a consistent rhythm to it? If so, reflect that in your playing by bringing out that rhythm, and using a chord sequence of an appropriate length.

(c) If a rhythm is established, this may help the singer to develop more of a song-like pattern, but if he starts to ignore the rhythm, allow the accompaniment to become more shapeless again. Let the singer lead, but always provide as much support as you can.

(d) Is the singer repeating a particular melodic phrase? If so, try to bring that out in your accompaniment.

(e) Has a call-and-response pattern developed? Some of the most powerful prophetic songs I have heard have involved the singer singing a line, which can then be repeated by the congregation. This helps to draw the congregation into what is going on. If this seems to be developing, be ready to lead the congregation by playing the notes they are to sing. They will soon recognise what you are doing, and will join in with you.

Playing an instrumental passage

At any of the above points, it may be fitting to play a chord sequence and/or melody of your own. Such a musical passage not only gives space for people to meditate or quietly sing and speak out their own worship; God can use it to open up hearts in a way that words cannot. Obviously, the structure of such a passage could be of any style and form, and we have already looked at some basic methods of approach. Be aware of what might be happening in the congregation, and keep an eye and ear out for any instruction or intervention by the leader.

All the above ideas can be integrated into a time of worship. Congregations may be unused to such expressions of the prophetic, and some may be confused, even alienated by it. A good way to keep congregations involved is to introduce a known worship song at the end of the prophetic passage that fits with the theme expressed, and which enables the people to join in.

Preparing for the improvised

Although all the above elements may be spontaneous, equally they could be worked out beforehand—God can inspire people before, as well as during, a service. Working out an accompaniment to a given reading enables both reader and musician to flow together. Gaps could be included during the reading that allow the congregation to reflect on the words as a musical passage is played. Similarly, a prophetic song may benefit from some preparation, both lyrically and musically. Such time does not detract from its inspiration.

In a more general sense, too, practice will help you to be more spontaneous. If you regularly accompany a singer who sings prophetically, you will build up a mutual understanding and sensitivity, and a chord sequence or melody stumbled across at home may suddenly spring to mind at an appropriate moment in the worship time. The fact that it didn't feel inspired when you first found it doesn't mean that its use in the service isn't.

Playing songs with prophetic insight

Finally, it's important to realise that we can bring prophetic interpretation to a worship time from within the songs themselves. Sometimes I find that when I am playing a particular song, a single phrase or line from the lyrics may jump out at me as something I feel God is wanting to home in on. Our songs often say many things, but sometimes the Lord wants to emphasise a specific idea or truth. I can draw attention to that particular line by building the song a little at that point, using some of the techniques we've been looking at. The effect can be overdone, of course, but if it is controlled, the music can encourage people to lift their spirits and focus their minds at that point, and so receive what God is saying. On a number of occasions I have seen God begin to move in power at that point, perhaps with the manifestation of other spiritual gifts as God leads.

In conclusion

I appreciate that many will feel a long way from being able to do the kinds of things outlined in this chapter. You may also feel that your church is light years away from it. Clearly you need to tailor what you do to fit within certain restrictions and limitations. But you can begin to implement creative elements, whatever stage your church is at. A musical accompaniment to a part of your regular liturgy, say, a Scripture reading, could be suggested, or you could write a new tune to a psalm or canticle, perhaps incorporating a call-and-response section.

Some elements of a congregation are always resistant to change. But when it comes to leaders in our churches, it is not so much the prospect of change, but the fear of things getting out of control that becomes the stumbling block. Many leaders simply need to be reassured of a sensitive approach to creative worship, perhaps working within the present liturgy, explaining clearly what would be involved, and so on. Clear communication will help avoid misunderstanding, and an open-hearted attitude on the part of the musician is more honouring to God than a belligerent approach which rides roughshod over the leader's sense of responsibility.

Chapter 6

PLAYING BY EAR

I will lead the blind by ways they have not known.
Isaiah 42:16

If there is one area of keyboard playing that gives some of us a massive inferiority complex, it is playing by ear. Songs which take us hours of dedicated practice to master are picked up effortlessly by others. We feel for ever slaves to our songbooks, while they sail through songs with consummate ease, having only heard the song through a couple of times, and they don't even need the music. And when required to improvise behind a Scripture reading, or invent an instrumental passage, they pluck out of the air beautiful chord sequences and memorable melodies, while we sit paralysed by fear, doggedly hammering out the only chord we can think of.

How do they do it? Is it a special technique, or sheer brilliance? Often these people cannot read a note of music, and yet their grasp of songs and musical hearing seems so much greater than ours. Is it a natural ability, or can it be learned?

Playing by sight and playing by ear

The gulf that seems to exist between those who can and those who can't play by ear springs from two very different approaches to keyboard playing. For many of us the process of learning to play the piano was a predominantly visual one: music was always written down, and often our progress was marked by how well we could read it. After many years of playing we might be highly skilled at converting what we see into notes on the piano, while our ability to convert what we hear remains grossly under-developed.

For the non-reader, the process has been quite the reverse. His musical ear is highly developed to recognise melodies and chord sequences as he hears them, and he can then reproduce them on the piano. He has developed a mental picture of how chords relate to one another, and can identify the chordal structure of a song, thus finding it easier to substitute chords and improvise within it.

The important point is that the distinction is one of self-training and familiarity, rather than of natural ability. True, some people undoubtedly have a flair and natural gifting for creative improvisation, but we can all train our ears to recognise notes and chords as they relate to one another, and so begin to play by ear, just as a non-reader can learn to become familiar with the lines, spaces and dots of written music.

Unfortunately, this chapter will not teach you to play by ear—it is not a comprehensive approach which will fit all the pieces together. Instead, I will present some ideas and exercises to get you started, and hopefully at some point down the road the penny will drop as you try things out for yourself.

Don't be put off by constant reference to chord numbers, intervals and so on. They only help to explain what is going on. When you learn a new language, you can feel overwhelmed by the lists of vocabulary, verbs and tenses, but with familiarity and practice the language becomes second nature, and you don't have to think quite so hard about it. The same is true of this process. With time you will recognise intervals between chords, and the process will be altogether more natural.

The process of playing by ear

There are two stages to the process. The first is hearing the music; the second is reproducing it on the keyboard. Now, although we may not be aware of it, most of us are very good at stage one.

If I suggest a tune—say, the national anthem—we can all run through it pretty accurately in our minds. Likewise, when someone strikes up the first note of 'Happy birthday', even the least musical folk can join in and sing it more or less perfectly. No one needs to know what key they are in, and no one needs to scramble for a copy of the music.

What is happening here? By a process of familiarity we have learned the melodic structure of a song—how the notes fit together to make a tune. We've probably never seen the music, and the song could have been started in any key, but we know how long each note is, and, more importantly, what the intervals are between the notes—how high or low to jump from one note to the next. Some of us may even be able to sing a harmony to the melody, showing an appreciation of which chords accompany the tune.

We should all take encouragement from knowing that the above process is actually a very complicated one! And yet we all do it so naturally using the musical instrument God has given us—our voices. Now translating this process onto the piano is going to be more difficult, simply because we're not as familiar with the keyboard as we are with our vocal chords; but essentially the process is the same.

EXERCISE ONE: For now, just try playing through 'Happy birthday' on the piano, singing it aloud at the same time. Begin on the note of D, and see if you can get to the end. If you can't find a particular note, keep playing the last note that was right and sing the note you can't find until, by trial and error, the notes you play match what you're singing.

Playing melodies by ear—recognising intervals

You've probably already realised that playing melodies by ear is a process of translating intervals between notes onto the keyboard. Although the key of a song can be varied, obviously the intervals don't change. One of the problems of being dependent on the written music of our songbooks is that we fail to appreciate intervals. For example, *Majesty* is written in G major, and hence we can't play it in any other key. But *Majesty* still remains *Majesty* in a different key, provided the intervals between the notes of the melody, and those between the chords, are retained.

What may have tripped you up in playing 'Happy birthday' is the fact that one of the notes is a sharp—the note in the first line, where we sing 'you', is an F♯. Now sharps and flats may tend to complicate things a little, but it is here that your knowledge of scales is going to come in very handy indeed.

Most of the songs we sing in church, based as they are on Western notions of harmony, will be written in a single key, and as such the notes of the melody are based on a single scale. (A few songs do change key, and quite a number of songs have melodies which modulate temporarily, but we shall deal with these in a moment.) If you know, for example, that you are playing in D major, your understanding of scales will tell you the eight notes to expect the melody to be based upon—including F♯ and C♯. Similarly, a song played in A major will include the notes of C♯, F♯ and G♯.

EXERCISE TWO: Taking a popular song, *Shine, Jesus, shine*, begin by singing it through. Keep time by tapping your left hand for each beat of the bar. Then try playing that on the piano (your songbook should be locked away somewhere for the duration of this chapter!). Play it through first in the key of A major, looking out for the sharpened notes of C, F and G. The first note of the melody is E. Sing as you play, so that you can feel with your voice how big the intervals are between notes, and you can better estimate them on the keyboard. And try it slowly at first, so you have time to think between notes.

Now try playing the same tune in a different key, say, G major. The G major scale includes one sharp, F, and the first note in the new key will be D. Try it through slowly, still singing as you play, and keeping time with your left hand.

Let's try the same thing with a different song: *Rejoice!*. Before playing through the melody, play the scale of D major in the right hand. Now play through the tune from memory: note that only notes from the D major scale are being used. Now play the scale of F major, noting the Bb. Play the melody through in this new key (the tune begins on a C), bearing in mind the notes of the F major scale to help you. To help you predict the intervals, again sing the tune as you play. (NB You will find that F major is a terrible key for singing this song!)

Try the same exercise with other songs, either from a songbook, or preferably from a familiar recording, or a song you know from memory. As you gain confidence, choose more unusual and difficult keys. Always play through the scale first, noting the various sharps or flats. If you do find you have to begin by working from songbooks, the sooner you can close the book and work it out by listening, the better.

Modulations within melodies

A modulation is simply a temporary key change within a song. In written music, it can often be spotted by the appearance of accidental sharps or flats appearing (or naturals in some keys). In this context, it may mean that some of the notes of the melody aren't in the scale you've been using.

EXERCISE THREE: Sing through *Spirit of the living God* (the 'break me, melt me' version). Notice how the note sung on 'mould' feels different the others. A modulation has happened here.

Try playing the song through, first in C major (the first note begins on E). Stop after playing 'melt me', and try to predict what the note will be for 'mould', Try to hear the interval between the note before and after it. It is this process of recognising intervals that will help you in playing melodies that modulate. (You don't need to know what key you are modulating into. It is enough to recognise the modulated notes in relation to the preceding and following notes. A glance at the chords will show you that the new key lasts just two bars.)

Try the song in different keys, using the same process as above to recognise the unusual note.

As intervals between notes become more and more familiar, you will begin to find that the process can work the other way round: playing along to a heard melody will help you find the key if you don't know it. Let's take an example. Someone at church begins a song quite spontaneously. You know the song, but you don't know what key they are singing in. By trial and error you find the note they are singing, and then you can work out each following note because you can hear the intervals between each note. You find you're playing several sharps, and in a few moments you recognise the scale of B major emerging. You play along to the rest of the song, confident in the knowledge you're in B major. (At a later point, you may then change the key if the singer has not chosen one suited to the congregation's singing range.)

Playing chords by ear

With practice, not only can we recognise and play intervals between notes, but also the relationship of chords to one another. Melodies are made up of notes of various intervals within a given key and scale. In the same way, songs are made up of chords in relation to one another, based upon a particular key.

We saw in Chapter 2 how a large number of songs are based upon the six chords within any given key: I, IIm, IIIm, IV, V, and VIm. So, for example, in *Rejoice!* (which is written in D major) the six chords would be D, Em, F♯m, G, A, and Bm. Now, not every song is quite so simple, but the important point is that songs all contain a chordal structure which, when understood, enables us to play that song in any key.

Let us take a song and look at it simply in terms of its chordal structure. *Abba Father* (SoF 1) is written in B♭ major in the songbook, but below are the chord numbers relative to whatever key we might choose to play the song:

I		IV		V		I	IV		V		I	

I   IV   V   I IV   V   I

Abba Father, let me be, Yours and Yours alone.

       IV V   I IV V   I

May my will for ever be, ever more Your own.

III VIm   III   VIm IIm   V

Never let my heart grow cold, never let me go.

I   IV   V   I IV   V   I

Abba Father, let me be, Yours and Yours alone.

EXERCISE FOUR: Try playing this song in the key of C major, using a simple style of chord in the right hand, and bass note in the left. Sing along, and play it slowly, as you work out each new chord. To get you started, the first line should be played like this:

C   F   G   C F   G   C

Abba Father, let me be, Yours and Yours alone.

Where I = C, IV = F and V = G. If you get stuck, simply count up from C to work out the chord, eg VIm in C would mean counting six up from C, and playing the minor chord, ie Am. When you have completed the song, try it again in a different key. Try this same exercise using a number of different songs. Write out the words, with the chord numbers over the top, and try playing the song in various keys.

The purpose of this exercise is twofold. First, by playing familiar songs in unusual keys, it helps to fix in your mind the families of chords associated with various keys. Knowing, for example, that the six related chords in the key of F♯ major are F♯, B, C♯, D♯m, G♯m and A♯m, and knowing how to play them, will equip you to cope with a song that by some terrible mishap ends up in that key during a worship time! Secondly, it begins to train your ear to recognise the relative positions of chords to each other. Intervals of, say, I to V, or IV to VIm will become familiar to your ears, so that you can recognise them in songs you are hearing for the first time, and ultimately you will be able to play those songs in any given key, because you have grasped the chordal structure.

This last point is the crux of being able to play by ear. If you were simply to cover your songbooks with roman numerals as a means of playing songs in different keys (which I don't recommend), and even if you then memorised them, you would simply be employing a process of memory and mathematics—it wouldn't be playing by ear. The next stage of the process is to learn to recognise the relations of chords to each other simply by hearing them.

The root note

Where do you begin? Well, the way to recognise any chord is to identify its root note—the note after which the chord is named. Chords are presented in different inversions, sometimes with additional notes, which only serve to confuse. And yet every chord has a foundational note, and if you can uncover this root note in each of a succession of chords, finding the relation between them will be as simple as recognising the intervals of a simple melody.

Recognising root notes

Unfortunately, there are no simple, universal rules for recognising root notes. And the more complex the chords, the harder it can be. However, simple three-note chords (or even four-note chords with, say, sevenths or seconds) should not present too many problems.

(a) *Familiarity with inversions.* As you looked at various inversions of chords in Chapter 2, you were encouraged to become familiar with them. You will find that continual use will train your ear to recognise the note of an inverted chord. Where you're not sure, use this simple test to check. As you hear or play an inversion, sing the note you think is the root. Now sing the first five notes of the scale that begins with that note. If you're right, the third and fifth of the scale should fit perfectly with the chord you're hearing/playing. If they don't, the note you're singing is probably not the root. (NB If the chord you're playing/hearing is minor, you must sing a minor scale—in other words, your ear needs to be able to distinguish between major and minor chords.)

(b) *The bass note.* The bass note (played in the left hand on the piano, or by the bass guitar) is sometimes helpful in finding the root note of a chord, as it is often the root note itself. In the above example of *Abba, Father*, all the bass notes are root notes, and therefore hearing the intervals between the chords could simply be a question of listening to the bass notes.

Unfortunately, the bass note is not always the root note, and it is worth using the scale test mentioned above to check on this. Get used to the sound of the bass note as the root note of the chord, eg D major with D in the bass, and compare it with chords where the bass note is not the root, eg D/F♯ or D/A. If you can begin to train your ear to recognise

94

when the root is and isn't in the bass (each of these three chords mentioned has a distinctive sound of its own), this will be very useful.

EXERCISE FIVE: Choose a chord, and play the root note in the bass left hand. Now play different inversions of the chord in the right hand, perhaps adding sevenths or even ninths. Note the distinctive sound, and make sure you can always pick out the root note irrespective of the inversion by singing it out loud. Try it with a series of different chords, major and minor.

Now change the bass note so that it is not the root of the chord. Note how the 'colour' of the chord changes, depending on whether the bass note is now the third or the fifth of the chord. Again, see if you can still sing the root note.

Finally, change the bass note again, this time to a note not contained in the right-hand chord, eg D major with C in the bass. Note how the sound of the chord has changed again. Once more see if you can sing the root note.

To recap

So what have we learned so far? We've seen that we all possess a certain natural ability to hear melodies and replay them, so to speak, with our voices, and that it's not such a big step to learn to replay them on a keyboard. Knowledge of scales is useful, and with a little time and effort we can become very quick at recognising even the more obscure intervals between notes.

Recognising chords can be more difficult, even though the actual chord structure of songs is usually far simpler than a melody. Difficulty comes because we are less used to hearing and handling chords. But again, as we persevere, we will suddenly recognise the intervals between chords because we can hear the relation of the chord's respective root notes.

Note how a combination of activities and approaches helps here. If you know the key you are in, you can have a pretty good idea of what chords to expect. Bass notes can give further clues as to the root notes, but you can't depend on the bass note being the root note.

As you become familiar with the sound of more complicated chords, ie, major sevenths, major ninths and beyond, you will begin to be able to recognise them when you hear them—I can usually recognise a complicated chord played by someone else, because I've already discovered it for myself by experimenting on the piano at home.

Further tips

1. Experiment with chords on your own, and it may remind you of songs and recordings you've heard before. It can be very exciting to stumble across the creative path of someone you've always admired!

2. Listen to Christian recordings of worship songs. In particular, listen to the keyboard part, and try to work out the particular chords and voicings being played. We can learn a lot from other people's creativity.

3. Modulations can be a problem: this is where a song steps out of its original key and moves into another one. In the above example of *Abba, Father*, the chord of III pops up in line three. We could be forgiven for expecting IIIm, which is one of the six related chords in our list. This unexpected chord definitely indicates a modulation into a different key—it sounds as though a harmonic change has happened, because the chord doesn't sound like it fits the original key.

If you can recognise when a modulation has happened during a song, at least then you're ready to explore a little further than the six related chords. Try to identify the root note of this unexpected chord in the way outlined above, bearing in mind that the bass note may help—in fact, the bass note is usually the best place to start. Then try to identify the nature of the chord—major, minor, any additional notes, and so on. And remember that modulations almost always revert to the original key after a few chords, so be on the lookout for the return of more familiar, expected chords.

Perfect pitch

Playing by ear is often associated with the ability known as 'perfect pitch'. This is the unusual gift of instantly being able to recognise the pitch of a note without the aid of any instrument. People with this ability seem to possess a kind of internal tuning fork against which they can recognise any given note.

Perfect pitch, although useful in itself, is not essential to playing by ear. What is required, and what this chapter is designed to develop, is 'relative pitch'; that is to say, given the name of a particular note, we can work out the name of another given note in relation to that one, by recognising the interval between them. We all have relative pitch to some extent, because when we are given the first note of a familiar song, we are able to sing the rest of that song in the same key.

In conclusion

This chapter is by no means a comprehensive guide to playing by ear—its aim is simply to go some way to explaining the processes behind this essentially aural approach to keyboard playing, and to encourage us all to develop our own musical ear accordingly. The exercises may stir you to explore for yourself, and give you a bigger picture of how this aspect of music actually works. For example, Exercise two, where we looked at the chordal structure of a song, might be a good model for recognising songs—far quicker and easier than learning arrangements note for note, and more flexible than learning the chords of a particular key. (Incidentally, this method of reading chord charts with numbers is common among many professional session players around the world, who might be called upon at any moment to play their song in any key.)

Chapter 7

CONTEMPORARY STYLES

Do not let your left hand know what your right hand is doing.
Matthew 6:3

One of the most daunting aspects of playing keyboards in worship these days is that of the contemporary style. Many a pianist who, when confronted with a Bach prelude and fugue would accept the task with an air of quiet confidence, actually begins to quake in terror at the prospect of *Jesus we celebrate Your victory!* The purpose of this chapter is to try to defuse some of this fear by looking at a few basic elements of the contemporary/popular sound, and how we can incorporate these elements into our playing.

It's interesting that, just as many contemporary keyboard players marvel at the way classical pianists convert that mass of dots on the page into beautiful music, so the classical player looks on in awe at the contemporary player's sense of rhythm and feel. And yet the difference between them is more to do with culture than ability. For my own part, as I grew up I listened to pop music which helped to shape my musical tastes and understanding. I was never taught it—it was regarded with disdain by my piano teacher—but it was integral to my aural musical education. If the pop culture hadn't existed then, or the predominant music in my home had been classical, my tastes would have developed very differently. We are all to some extent products of our upbringing in this respect.

That doesn't mean that a 'pop' education is preferable or more desirable than any other. But we need to understand that many of the worship songwriters who have come to prominence in recent years have been more influenced by pop and rock than by classical music. Writing with guitar rather than piano, many of them now work regularly with worship bands that use drums, bass, electric guitars and synthesisers, and this further influences their writing.

Pop music may not be your cup of tea, but if you can get to grips with a few of its elements, we will be able to handle most things that are thrown at you in even the most contemporary times of worship.

Elements of the contemporary sound

We are all aware that rhythm plays an important part in pop/rock. The most basic element of this is the particular beats of the bar we emphasise. Classical training may have taught us that in a four-beat bar, the beats to emphasise are one and three. In contemporary music, however, the accented beats are usually two and four.

Listen to the drum pattern in a contemporary-style recording (Christian or secular): the most distinctive sound is the crack of the snare drum, which in a 4/4 song is most likely being played on the off-beats. Clap along to it. Then try clapping on beats one and three. Doesn't have the same effect, does it?

So one aspect of the contemporary sound is the strong emphasis on beats two and four. However, you may also have noticed that beats one and three are not being completely ignored. In fact, the most likely thing you hear on these beats is the deep sound of the bass guitar and bass drum. Just as the snare tends to emphasise off-beats, so the bass instruments handle the front end and middle of the bar.

Try out the following rhythm with your hands. Hit your thigh with your left hand, and a table-top, or some other brighter-sounding object, with your right. Then with your mouth imitate the drum's hi-hat sound by making a short 't' sound.

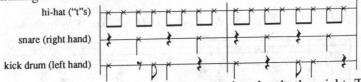

Do this slowly at first to ensure you are getting the rhythm right. Then gradually speed it up. This is the archetypal contemporary rock rhythm.

Let us translate this to the keyboard. We can use our left/right hand in a bass/snare rhythm which imitates the modern drum kit:

99

This is obviously a very simple example, but the contemporary elements are there. You will find that the right hand will begin to move away from being tied to the snare pattern, and become more complex, following some of the emphases of the hi-hat pattern. Note, however, that the left hand must remain relatively steady, and acts as the anchor; the stable emphasis which makes sense of the more intricate right-hand rhythms.

The right hand needn't be tied exclusively to the snare, of course. It has other jobs to do, such as providing some chordal backing for the rest of the bar. But irrespective of what else you're playing, in order to maintain that rock feel you may have to give regular emphasis to that snare beat by hitting it harder (this only really applies if you're not playing with drums).

For many of us, developing a degree of rhythmic independence between left and right hands will take a lot of practice. In the following exercises, concentrate on working the rhythms in the right hand around a steady left-hand bass line. Use the left hand as the steadying influence. You may find it helpful to use a metronome or drum machine to help you with this, as the tendency is to speed up, or to lose the steady sense of rhythm:

In the early stages of learning these rhythms, start by ignoring what is written in the left hand completely. Just play the note of C in the left hand on each beat of the bar, so:

This will help you to establish the beats of the bar in your head. Only when you feel ready, start playing the left hand as written. Even then start by playing the left hand on its own, and gradually add in the right hand.

Try playing these through very slowly at first, so that you can fit all the rhythms together. Count aloud the numbers above the stave, 'one-and-two-and', as this will help you. At all times try to keep the rhythm going, no matter how slowly you have to do it, and then, as you gain confidence, gradually speed it up to a comfortable pace.

If this kind of rhythm is new to you, don't expect to master it after a few minutes. This is the beginning of a long process of teaching your left and right hands to interact rhythmically. See how some of the notes are kept short, to increase the rhythmic feel, and feel how in some places one hand comes off as the other comes on. These are all quite tricky nuances, but perseverance will bring its reward.

As you progress, try playing different chords to the same rhythm, and do it from memory. You can then even invent your own rhythms by shifting the right hand to a different off-beat. Remember at all times to keep the left hand steady and solid.

If you feel depressed at this point by your inability to master these quickly, don't give up hope. Some of these rhythms are quite complicated, and it does take a long time to make them sound really good. It's generally helpful to bear in mind that we tend to rush syncopation a little, so try to hold it back if you can. It needs to be as steady as a rock, and yet bright and confident. Don't be afraid to hit the chords quite hard.

This kind of syncopation can be found in a number of recent worship songs. Take, for example, the common introduction/turn-round figure for *There is power in the name of Jesus* (SoF 545):

The figure, although not particularly complex, is a little tricky to play in time. So to help us, we could introduce a steady bass line as we have seen, such as this:

But perhaps an even easier place to begin is to make the left hand more metronome-like:

The left hand gives us a solid quaver foundation into which we can fit the syncopated right hand. Try the two hands together slowly at first, concentrating particularly on the syncopated right hand, and which note it plays with in the left hand, so:

As you increase the speed, make sure the left-hand quavers are rock steady as far as timing is concerned. The temptation will be to rush them where the syncopation occurs.

Syncopation is particularly common in the melody of a lot of contemporary-style songs. Here we need to be careful, as the tendency might be to make our left-hand accompaniment follow the melody, when in fact the rhythm of the accompaniment should be left unsyncopated.

A common example of this is with *Jesus, we celebrate Your victory*.

The melody

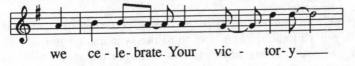

should not be followed rhythmically by the bass of the left hand, or (unless playing the melody) by the right hand. Hence, as the left hand is following a pattern of

it should continue unbroken through the syncopated melody.

Anticipation or 'push'

Sometimes the accompaniment does need to follow the melody in emphasising an unusual place in the bar. The most common circumstances for this is known as a 'push', where the accent anticipates the first beat of the bar. See *Lord of lords* below (SoF 361):

In the first two bars the tune is syncopated, but the left hand remains steady. However, in bars three and four ('Glo -' and 'God') both melody and accompaniment anticipate the first beat of the following bar. Now, the tendency for some players is to lose their sense of timing and actually cut parts of beats out, but we need to understand that a push does not cut anything out; it simply lays the emphasis on a different place within the bar.

Try playing this passage through slowly, counting 'one-and-two-and' as you go. This should help you to fit the syncopation into the correct timing without cutting anything out. Pay particular attention to the 'four-and-one-and-two' across bars 3 and 4, as the chord comes on that last 'and', and is sustained through to the 'two'. The metronome may come in useful here, to ensure all the beats are the right length.

Syncopation, of course, is not limited to contemporary rock songs, as this example from Graham Kendrick's *Restore, O Lord* (SoF 483) reveals (see following page).

We saw back in Chapter 1 how certain songs need some kind of fill to help keep all the beats the full length. The secret is to count through each bar (out loud, at first), so no beats are cut from the long-held note ('God'), and no speeding up occurs.

Emphasis and syncopation are perhaps the two fundamentals of achieving a more contemporary sound in our playing, along with the solid, single-note (or octave) left hand and chordal work of the right hand. It may take some time to develop the skill of a syncopated right

to the liv - ing God,—— whose king - dom

hand and steady left-hand interaction, but press on! The thing to keep bearing in mind is that most of us rush the syncopation. Make a conscious effort to hold back syncopated sections, and you will probably find you keep better time. Use of a metronome or drum machine again gives you something to judge yourself against.

'Gospel' styles of playing

So far we have only alluded to a more rock-orientated style of playing. And yet gospel, or Black gospel, is one of the most popular and aspired-to styles of playing keyboards, having had an influence on just about every contemporary style of music. Unfortunately, it is also one of the most difficult.

Some of the rock elements we have already examined appear in gospel, but in addition to an emphasis on half-beats, it also sometimes uses quarter-beats, like this:

(The way I suggest you count this is to count the *quaver* beats rather than the crotchets, up to a total of eight, as written above the stave.)

However, what is central to making this style work is an element of feel and timing that can't really be defined. It's too minute to write down in notation, and yet it makes all the difference. One way of understanding it is to think of the quarter beats as being themselves split up into triplets, thus:

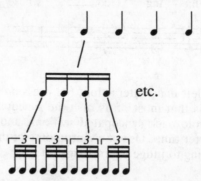

Understand that this is more descriptive of a feel than an accurate analysis, but it might be possible for some of you to develop this kind of style.

There are certain other elements that come into the category of gospel. One is the use of octaves to play a short riff, as in the example above, at the end of the first bar. Another is the grace note, where one of the notes of the bar is preceded by a light, short note, often a semitone down, that 'slides' into it:

The grace note is very short, and the effect should be very smooth and hardly noticeable—it adds a kind of slurring effect. This needs lots of practice otherwise it can sound heavy-handed and clumsy, or too staccato.

Yet another effect is one often associated with the 'blues', the tension of the major/minor third in the chord. Gospel plays on a similar idea, interchanging between major and minor.

Back in Chapter 1 we were looking at Dave Bilbrough's song, *O, the joy of Your forgiveness* (p 20). We came across the chord of D7♯9 which, if you look closely, effectively contains both the major and the minor third (♯9 = minor third)! In gospel you may also find that the two are used interchangeably, with the major third chords for the sweeter sections, then reverting to the minor third chord for a heavier feel.

One of the most noticeable aspects of gospel is its use of thick, rich chords, which help to give individual gospel players their distinctive styles. But it's up to you to experiment for yourself: this isn't an 'instant-gospel' kit!

Increasingly, other musical influences are beginning to show themselves, both in the way songs are written, and in how they are arranged for recordings and live use. We can't begin to cover all of them here, but I've selected a couple of the more common ones for examination below.

It is important to appreciate that what and how you play should be tailored to the other instruments you're playing with. For example, playing with a drummer and a bass player obviously frees you from having to anchor the rhythm on keyboards. In the examples below I've assumed you're playing more or less on your own, so if you are playing with others, cut down what you play.

Latin rhythms

'Latin' covers a whole range of different rhythms and accents, but again it's one that depends on a solid bass-end rhythm around which everything else works. One regular feature of Latin worship songs is the anticipation, or 'push', of one or both the off-beats. Instead of the rock style of emphasising beats two and four, thus:

the accent on the fourth beat is brought forward to beat three-and-a-half:

eg, *O taste and see* (SoF 447):

One of the most problematic of Latin fiesta-style songs is Graham Kendrick's *The trumpets sound (The feast is ready)* (SoF 550), because of the difficult piano intro. In the first two bars, the off-beat is pushed in two places, as indicated (see top of following page).

But I think the main problem comes in the fact that the bass line is also pushed in two places (indicated by the tied notes). The arrangement as it stands leaves you with very little to base your 'pushes' around, if you have no drummer to set out clearly where the beats are. One way to simplify and steady the piano part is to miss out both of the ties (see second example on following page).

After some practice, you may find you can reintroduce the ties without losing your sense of rhythm, but it works quite well (some would argue *better*) without them. In fact making sure the left hand

plays a note on the first beat of every bar is a useful technique through-out the song.

In all these Latin rhythms, note how keeping the accented note short, ie using quavers, adds to the rhythmic feel. These kinds of rhythms take a little practice to become comfortable with, but once you begin to explore this interaction of left and right hand, you can begin to experiment for yourself, and discover the many variations possible on the Latin theme.

Swing rhythms

Some songs, although written in a 3/4 or 4/4 time, definitely have an integral swing rhythm. Sometimes this is indicated by the guide word at the top of the arrangement, and a case in point is *Jesus, You are the radiance* (SoF 312). This is described as a 'light jazz waltz style', but other terms that imply the same feel are 'in a swing time', or occasionally 'in a dixieland style' (*The Lord has led forth His people with joy* makes for great dixieland!).

This feel involves the use of triplets. Instead of each crotchet beat being divided into two quavers like this:

it's divided into triplets, thus:

Swing usually emphasises the first and third of these triplets, so the swing rhythm is thought of as this:

For a song in 4/4 time, it may be helpful to count it as a 12/8 song, or as in the case of *Jesus, You are the radiance*, a 3/4 song in 9/8 time:

In conclusion

Regrettably we can only scratch the surface of these contemporary styles within the confines of a book such as this; and inevitably we have had to caricature somewhat crudely some of the styles and feels it takes year of dedicated playing to master. Nevertheless, I hope you are left with some pointers as to how to experiment and develop your own playing. This chapter may not turn you into an Andrae Crouch or a Leon Patillo overnight, but it may help you get to grips with some difficult songs.

Chapter 8

THE WORLD OF SYNTHESISERS

You hear its sound but cannot tell where it comes from.
John 3:8

If you think that the whole area of keyboards has changed a lot within the church over the last fifteen years, it's nothing in comparison with what's been happening outside. In the world of pop music, the swing from the guitar-based sound of the sixties to the more synthesiser-influenced sound of the seventies is clear. However, the eighties brought with them a technical revolution that has transformed the recording industry and the whole sphere of popular music for ever. Synthesisers, samplers, MIDI and digital recording are the buzz-words of this revolution that has spawned a bewildering number of keyboards, which in turn are capable of creating a breathtaking variety of sounds. And the revolution continues.

The problem with discussing the technology in any detail is that any comments or recommendations almost immediately become outdated; keyboards are replaced by other keyboards that do the job better and cost less, and unless you really know what you want, you can easily feel overwhelmed by the whole thing. The purpose of this chapter, therefore, is to make some general points about the technology that give you some background knowledge, and should help you when it comes to buying equipment.

Look—no strings!

The main reason many of us are cautious about synthesisers is twofold; first, the feel of the keyboard often seems 'cheap' and un-piano like; second, synthesisers that purport to sound like, say, a real piano, do nothing of the sort. However, it is now possible to buy keyboards that sound and feel pretty much like a real piano. It's taken a surprisingly long time (given the pace of technological advance), but there are now keyboards in existence whose sound can (and often does) fool most people. Such 'digital' pianos (as they are sometimes called) have certain obvious advantages over the acoustic strung variety: they're more portable, they require little or no maintenance, they don't go out of tune, the overall volume is easily adjustable, and they plug straight into a public address amplification system. One disadvantage is that most do need some kind of amplifier and loudspeaker, whether that's a full-blown PA system or a little portable amplifier/loudspeaker 'combo'.

One other advantage of the digital piano is the range of piano sounds on it. Arguably none of the 'authentic' piano sounds offer the flexibility or dynamic range of a real piano (although some come close), but you may find there are other sounds available on the same instrument that help to offer you some dynamic alternatives as compensation.

Aside from the piano sound, the most common basic keyboard sound used in worship is the electric piano, or 'rhodes' sound. Less percussive, softer and more bell-like, this sound is in its element when used as a simple sustained chordal 'pad', undergirding the rest of the worship band sound. It works on its own too in more intimate moments of worship, or when other things are going on top of it—prophecies, Scripture readings, and so on. The sound often comes with a 'chorus' effect (which in stereo can sound enormous!) helping to thicken out the sound further. Beware of playing too many low notes at the same time when playing in a band, though, as you can 'muddy' the sound somewhat.

Other keyboards are capable of creating just about any sound you might wish for. Between them, synthesisers and samplers (which use the same reproductive technology as compact discs) can produce rich string orchestras, bright brass, ethereal vocal sounds, electric or acoustic guitars, cathedral organs, flutes, percussion—virtually anything is possible. But before you rush out and buy enough equipment to replace the rest of your music group, it may be worth looking at their strengths and weaknesses in the worship setting.

Synthesisers in worship

Care is needed in how various sounds are used. For a start, we may have to be honest with ourselves and admit that 'alien spaceships landing' is a preset facility which will probably not be appropriate in any worship context. Piano, electric piano (sometimes called 'rhodes') and organ sounds have obvious applications, and can be played as any acoustic piano. However, sounds that imitate other real instruments need to be played in a manner befitting the instrument; flutes, for example, play single notes within a certain range, and huge ten-fingered chords using that sound will sound odd. Similarly, a brass sound might be effective as a fanfare in three-part harmony during the chorus, but played across the keyboard throughout the whole song will sound brash and overpowering. Always keep in mind the instrument you're imitating.

Some sounds do not directly imitate one particular instrument, but it is still important to assess carefully how the sound can best be used. In what range of the keyboard does the sound work—high, low, in the middle? How thick is the sound? Thick sounds may only need one note playing at a time. If you are playing with a music group, will it clash with other instruments? The general rule to follow is, be sparing. Sounds and musical figures are made most effective by limiting their use. And remember, other solo instruments need room to play, so don't squeeze them out by filling every space with your musical ideas.

The most common synthesiser sound I use is a rich, subtle string sound, which I play at a low level behind a piano or electric piano sound. It fills out the general sound without being obtrusive, and by fading it in and out at various sections, it brings new 'colours' to the song by highlighting, say, the chorus, or the second verse.

Having read the ground-rules, however, feel free to be creative! There are so many possibilities, and the power of a song can be greatly added to by creative and sensitive use of synthesisers.

Some practical ideas on synthesiser playing

Simply because a synthesiser can imitate so many different instruments, as well as create a whole range of sounds unique to itself, you need to utilise your arranging skills to the full if you are to use the sounds effectively. As you page through the different sounds on your synth, try to imagine it in the context of the overall worship band sound. Could you hear this or that sound fitting in well? You probably need to try it out in rehearsal before you unleash it on a Sunday morning! Also ask yourself what sort of mood the sound creates.

Bright brassy sounds

Useful in short bursts in more up-tempo songs, as a contemporary brass section might be used, or for more fanfare-like effects. Look for short riffs, either single notes in octaves, or in three-part harmony. Don't sustain the notes for any length of time, as the sounds can be a little synthetic, and don't play across the melody, as the sound will easily overpower the tune. Be very sparing in its use, as the ear very quickly tires of such a strong sound.

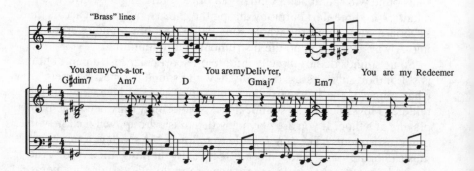

Warm brassy sounds

Very effective in three-part harmony, either as a riff or following the tune. A few sustained notes will work, but again try to imagine what a real brass section might play—fairly short phrases rather than long-held notes across the whole song. Above all, don't play this sound as you would a piano, as the authenticity of the sound will be lost.

Soft pads

This includes warm, synthy string sounds, as well as breathy or 'voicey' sounds. Very useful as a pad to undergird the overall sound. Unobtrusive, and as such lends itself to being MIDI'd up to a piano or rhodes sound, and played as such. (See below for a discussion of MIDI.) These sounds can be a little 'boomy', so don't play low notes, and EQ the sound if you can. (Many synths have built-in adjustable EQ, or better still, something called 'keyboard scaling', which allows you to decrease the volume of the sound, the further down—or up—the keyboard you go.)

Remember, you can heighten a pad's effectiveness by not using it all the way through a song. Leave it out of, say, the first verse and chorus, and then introduce it in verse two, increasing its volume in the chorus; then pull it out again for verse three, and so on.

Bells

The softer bell sounds are good for playing short single-note riffs around the tune, or for playing parts of the tune itself, sometimes. Again, don't overdo it, as it then begins to lose its effect.

The stronger, more authentic, bell sound needs more care and subtlety. It has its place, of course, in the right context, but be very sparing in its use, or you might sound like a grandfather clock, or a psychotic campanologist barricaded in the bell-tower.

Organ

This falls into two categories: the more traditional 'stops' variety, and the 'hammond'-type sound so beloved by sixties pop groups and black gospel churches. It's rare to find a synthesiser that can imitate anything like the range of sound possible on a full-blown church organ, and although an adequate backdrop sound can usually be found on a synth, don't get into hot water by trying to replace the real thing, if the latter is operational in your church!

The hammond sound works very well in a range of songs. Its strength is that, like other genuine keyboard sounds, it carries the whole range of styles and techniques possible on a keyboard—single-note riffs around the tune, chordal accompaniment, or more rhythmically. But once again, heighten its effectiveness by using it sparingly if it is not the central keyboard sound. The occasional glissando is also effective—that is to say, running a finger (or in this case a whole hand is better!) from the bottom of the keyboard up to a chord, so:

You may come across other sounds that don't fit into any of the above categories. If they resemble other instruments, use them as such; if they don't, take time to examine their texture and brightness, so you can use them sensitively. And please bear in mind that even if you do have a wonderful flute sound, and you do play it well, it may not be particularly discreet to use it if you already have a real flute in your worship group! Of course, you could work out parts together, playing harmonies, perhaps; but it pays to be sensitive in your use of imitative sounds.

The wonderful world...of MIDI

If you have had any contact with electronic keyboards of any kind, you will probably have come across the term 'MIDI'. It may only signify three strange-looking sockets in the back of your synthesiser, but it's actually a very useful piece of technology that has revolutionised the music world.

MIDI—Musical Instrument Digital Interface—is a system by which electronic instruments (and computers) can communicate with each other. Simply plug two machines together, and they can pass between them all sorts of information about what is being played. The most common practical application for us as musicians is that it enables us to play several keyboards at once—with only one pair of hands! As we hit notes on one keyboard, the other keyboards are told to play exactly the same thing as the first, using their own programmed sounds.

This has a number of useful advantages. First, you can 'stack' a number of sounds together from different synthesisers, all triggered from one keyboard, creating a rich blend of sounds (bear in mind, however, what we have discussed about the appropriate use of sounds). Second, you need only deal with one physical keyboard, and yet have access to any number of sounds from different machines. In fact, increasingly it is possible to buy synthesiser 'sound modules'—synthesisers with no physical keyboard at all, whose sounds can be triggered via MIDI from another synthesiser with a keyboard. They tend to be cheaper than their keyboard equivalent, and obviously take up less space, often coming in the form of a thin black box. (For more on the ins and outs of MIDI, see the glossary.)

Conversely, just as you can buy a box of sounds without a keyboard, so you can buy a keyboard without sounds! Finding a synthesiser which has the sounds you like and a keyboard that feels right can be a problem. A master or 'mother' keyboard makes no sounds, but the physical keyboard is usually very well made, and feels very much like a real piano. Obviously you need to buy sound modules actually to make the sounds, but if the feel of the keyboard is important to you, it may be worth finding a master keyboard that you really enjoy playing. Having said that, some synthesisers do have good keyboards already, so it's worth trying different ones out.

The keyboard action

What do you look for in a good keyboard? Different players have different tastes, and you need to find one that suits your style, as you would with any acoustic piano. Most reasonable keyboards these days are velocity sensitive; that is to say, the harder you hit a note, the louder it will sound. In addition, if you are essentially a pianist, you may prefer the piano-like feel of weighted keys to a synthesiser keyboard action, but remember, they do cost more, and they tend to be far heavier. Some compromise may be needed if portability is an important factor.

Keyboards do come in different sizes. Standard synthesisers have sixty-one notes, while the two larger sizes are seventy-six and eighty-eight notes (the latter being closest to the size of a standard acoustic piano). Keyboards with weighted keys tend to come in the latter two sizes, and if your intention is primarily to play in a piano-style with piano sounds, you may find the limited range of the smallest size too restrictive.

Purchasing keyboard equipment

Because of the changing nature of the technology available, it is difficult to be specific about buying equipment. However, there are a few general principles you can follow to help you find what you need.

(a) Find a helpful music shop. Assistants are there to help you and answer any queries you might have, no matter how simple. Don't be put off by a shop's exclusive appearance or customers.

(b) Don't be afraid to shop around. It's a competitive market for retailers, because of the money involved, and looking at various outlets could result in you saving quite a lot of money. Keyboard magazines (available at many newsagents) are often a good place to find out a competitive price for a particular item of equipment, once you know what you want. Often you can order equipment by direct mail-order from advertisements in these magazines, or alternatively you can bargain with your local shop.

(c) When looking at synthesisers with a physical keyboard, or master keyboard, spend time finding one that you're comfortable playing. Very cheap ones can be attractive because of the price tag, but if they're not velocity sensitive, ultimately it will be frustrating trying to play expressively on it. A good keyboard action will give you pleasure for years, and you can always update your sounds by buying sound modules.

(d) On the subject of modules (sometimes called 'rack-mount' synthesisers), be realistic about what you buy, particularly if it is predominantly for use in worship. You can spend large sums on impressive modules that contain weird and wonderful sounds you'll never use, when all you need is good string and brass sounds which will cost you far less.

(e) When budgeting for equipment, remember that you'll need more than just the keyboard. A sustain pedal, a keyboard stand, an amplifier and leads, and preferably a flightcase for protection purposes will all be necessary, and these may run into hundreds of pounds extra. Allow for these essentials in your calculations.

(f) In addition to new equipment, there is a thriving second-hand market in keyboards. A free classified section can be found in the back of most keyboard magazines, where prices are appreciably lower. The dangers of second-hand purchases apply here as anywhere else, but generally speaking, this kind of equipment is sufficiently well made to last many years. Actual keyboards, which obviously have more mechanical parts, need closer inspection.

In conclusion

The world of keyboards and keyboard purchasing is not cheap—you may find yourself wishing you'd stuck to the recorder! It is worth finding out if your church could help out financially, and, if not, think up ways you and your music group could raise money. Good keyboards are a blessing to church worship (as any church with a £20,000 organ restoration fund will tell you).

Appendix 1

Playing with Others

Although we have covered a number of areas in this book, we've tended to look at the keyboard as an instrument in isolation. The subject of playing with others is another book in itself, but we can give a little thought to it here for those who find themselves playing in worship with other instruments.

We have already seen that many of us need to simplify our playing style. When playing with others this becomes absolutely crucial—and will take a lot of discipline. You may be used to providing an accompaniment which incorporates melody, harmony and rhythm all rolled into one. You play according to your own rules, using, if not the full range of the keyboard, at least a large part of it, and at a pace that fluctuates according to how you feel about the song. Suddenly, when other instruments are added in, everything begins to sound messy and unclear. It doesn't sound as though you are all playing *together*, and it certainly doesn't sound like it does on the worship albums.

You may not realise it, but the problem is with you. You haven't really changed your style to accommodate other instruments, and so you are in effect doubling everything that the other instruments are doing— and probably not very accurately!

It is best to begin by understanding what the different individual instruments in your worship group contribute. For example, if you play with drums, the drummer's role is to set the pace and basic rhythmic feel of a song. You need to play at *his* speed—listening in particular to the hi-hat, which will be emphasising the quaver or semi-quaver beats. *Your* quavers need to fit into that pattern and not race ahead of it.

Similarly, if you play with a bass guitar, you need to leave out the notes at the bottom end of the keyboard—play single notes in the left hand rather than octaves, and generally keep it above the C two octaves below middle C. In fact, it's a useful exercise to play for a while with your right hand only, missing out the bass altogether. You will probably find the bottom end of the sound of your group then becomes much clearer and better defined.

Again, if you play with solo instruments who improvise around the melody lines, you need to be very sparing in your own 'fills', so that they have space in which to work. Your constant arpeggios will obscure their contribution, and make for a rather muddy overall sound. Even when they are not playing, keep your own playing minimal and notice how pleasant it is to have a little space in the overall sound.

So what is there left for the keyboard player to play? Well, as we have seen earlier in the book, a simple, sustained chord, only moving when the chord changes, is often all that is needed. It provides a good, solid foundation and helps to warm up the overall sound. A sustained chord has a beauty all its own, particularly if played on a well-chosen synthesiser sound, or if the chord has a slight embellishment on the straight three-note chord. It then also leaves the other instruments free to make their contribution.

Sometimes a worship group may be weak in one of the three areas outlined—melody, harmony or rhythm—and in this instance the keyboard may be required to compensate for that weakness. If, for example, there is no bass guitar in the group, the keyboard player should then be conscious of filling the gap by playing fairly deep bass notes, as a bass guitar would. Similarly, a lack of drums or percussion should cause the keyboard player to think a little more rhythmically. However, a strummed acoustic guitar can provide a strong, rhythmic foundation on its own as it emphasises the quaver or semi-quaver beats, and the keyboard doesn't need to double it.

In short, since the keyboard is arguably the most flexible of the instruments used in worship, keyboard players too should be the most versatile of all musicians. The old adage that 'less is more' holds true, and playing *simply and accurately* is an art in itself. You should be compensating for any weaknesses in the sound, leaving space for others, sometimes simply leaving space, and 'locking in' to the rhythmic foundation of drums or acoustic guitar. If these principles are followed, your worship group and your church will reap the benefits of your controlled playing.

Finally, may I encourage you to listen carefully to professional musicians playing on all kinds of albums, but particularly worship albums. Listen to what the keyboards are playing, the kind of sounds being used, the kind of chords played, where fills are put in, where space is left, and so on. Try to imitate some of these styles in your own playing, and you will find that this will begin to influence your own style for the better.

Appendix 2

Chords Reference Section

All the following chords are based on the key of C for simplicity. I've tended not to use root positions, but good-sounding inversions: however, the choice of inversion you use is, of course, yours. I've chosen just a few of the most common chords you'll come across.

The notes of the staves

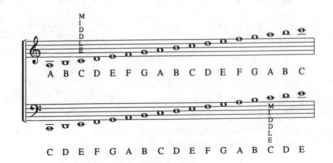

Major

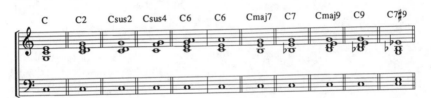

Minor

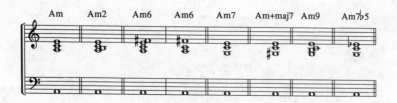

Dim/aug

Glossary

a cappella Unaccompanied singing.

action What it feels like to play a keyboard. A weighted action is heavier to play than a synthesiser action (and many keyboard players prefer it). But the action of a keyboard varies considerably from make to make, and prospective purchasers should take time to find a keyboard with an action that suits them.

arpeggio The playing of the notes of a chord one after another in a quaver or semi-quaver pattern, rather than simultaneously. Excessive or constant arpeggio playing should be avoided.

bridge A section in a song that links the verse to the chorus. Not that common in worship songs, which consist mostly of just two sections—verse and chorus.

chord chart A simple way of writing out songs without using staves, but based on the chords of the song. Some people mistakenly assume chord charts are for guitarists only, and must use the little guitar 'finger shape' symbols often seen in guitar manuals. But chord charts are just as useful for keyboard players, and consist simply of the chord names, written out in such a way as to show where they are to be played in the bar.

chord progression A series of chords that fit together to create a dynamic effect.

circle of 5ths A phenomenon in Western harmony that enables the player to move through all the major/minor chords by stepping down five notes every time. It can help in finding chords with which to change key smoothly.

combo An amplifier with a built-in speaker, essential for hearing your own electronic keyboard if it does not possess its own internal speakers—unless of course you are plugging straight into the church PA system.

dominant The 5th note of the scale, or the 5th chord in the key, denoted throughout this book by a V.

dynamics The elements of playing that bring feeling and emotion to a song: loudness and softness, strident playing and light gentleness, changing pace. These are just some of the elements that come under the umbrella of dynamics.

fill A term used to describe a series of notes that fill in between chords. They add interest to the keyboard part, but care must be taken not to obscure either the tune or the playing of some other instrument. When the keyboard alone is playing a fill may help to maintain the speed of a song in between lines, thus preventing a congregation from coming in too early with the next line.

foldback/monitors PA systems offer many advantages to a worship group, enabling all the instruments and voices to be heard by the congregation. However, PA speakers tend to be pointed at the congregation and away from the musicians, which makes it difficult for musicians to hear each other or even themselves. Foldback speakers are smaller units placed on the floor, pointing towards the musicians, and they feed some of the PA sound back to those who are making it! Foldback is particularly import-ant for singers, who need to hear themselves in order to sing in tune, and yet often can't if they are standing in front of a loud rhythm section.

half time A device used in contemporary music when the rhythm accom-paniment, instead of emphasising beats two and four, emphasises beat three, and so gives the impression of playing at half the original speed. (The speed of the melody doesn't change, of course.)

intro Introduction.

inversions Ways of playing a chord without the root note at the bottom of the chord (see **root position**). A simple three-note chord such as D major has two possible inversions—F♯ at the bottom, A in the middle, and the D at the top (1st inversion); and A at the bottom, D in the middle and F♯ at the top (2nd inversion). Four-note chords, eg Dmaj⁷, will have three inversions, etc. Being familiar with inversions enables chords to be played in smooth progression, as the fingers move smoothly to adjacent notes.

mid 8 A section of a song that appears for the first time after a number of times through the verse and chorus (or verse, bridge and chorus). Very common in modern secular songs, but still quite unusual in the predomi-nantly verse-chorus format of worship songs. Although the phrase refers to the middle eight bars of a song, the actual number of bars can vary.

MIDI Musical Instrument Digital Interface. An electronic system that is standard to virtually all electronic keyboards. By use of a simple connect-ing lead, keyboards (and computers) can communicate with each other so that, for example, a player can operate any number of synthesisers from a single keyboard.

MIDI channel There are sixteen MIDI channels (numbered 1-16), enabling a player to control a large number of modules from a single keyboard. It is important to ensure that the 'MIDI Send' channel of the master keyboard tallies with the 'MIDI receive' channel of the module, or no sound will be produced (probably the most common cause of confusion among keyboard players!)

If you have, say, one master keyboard, and three modules that you want to produce sounds simultaneously, simply set the master keyboard to, say, 'MIDI send' channel 1, and the 'MIDI receive' of the modules to the same number (see fig. 1 below). If however you want to play each module on its own at different points in a song, set the 'MIDI receive' channels to three different numbers, say 1, 2 and 3. Set the master keyboard 'MIDI send' to channel 1 for the first sound, then change it quickly to 2 for the second sound, and so on.

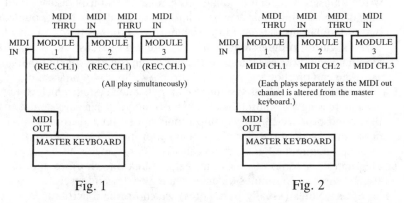

Fig. 1   Fig. 2

When plugging in MIDI leads, bear in mind where the MIDI information is going from, and where it's going to. You are sending information from the master keyboard, so your first lead needs to come out of the master's MIDI OUT socket. It's then going into module 1, so the other end of the lead goes into module 1's MIDI IN socket. Now, here is where you have to think. The same information that went into module 1, you want to go into module 2, so the next lead needs to go from module 1's MIDI THRU to module 2's MIDI IN socket. Likewise the final lead needs to go from module 2's MIDI THRU socket to module 3's MIDI IN socket. (The module's MIDI OUT sockets aren't used, because the modules are not generating any MIDI information of their own.) Remember that each module will only recognise MIDI information if it is set to the right 'MIDI receive' channel. So if you only want to play module 2, for example, set the master keyboard to 'MIDI send 2', and module 1 will ignore the information and simply pass it through its MIDI THRU socket to module 2. There is no need to bypass module 1 with the leads. (See figure 2 above.)

MIDI can at first be slightly complex to work with, but its advantages and even enormous potential will soon be evidence. It should be borne in mind, however, that MIDI has nothing to do with the actual audio or sound signal that goes to an amplifier or PA system: it is simply a way of passing note information. You will need to plug each of the modules into the mixing desk or amplifier with jack leads, and control the sound from there.

module A 'keyboard' with no actual physical keyboard, just the sounds. It can be played via MIDI from another keyboard.

modulation A section within a song where the key seems to change: often recognisable by the appearance of chords you would not expect in the original key, and the appearance of sharps or flats (or naturals) in the written music. Although modulations can be temporarily disorientating, they do usually find their way back into the original key after a couple of bars. Modulations present most problems when one is trying to play by ear, as chord progressions can be quite unusual as the song first modulates, and the ear may not be used to the sound of the intervals.

outro The end of a song.

PA system Public Address system. An amplification system which is being used increasingly in churches. One big advantage of such a system is that the sound produced by a worship group can be 'mixed' from a mixing desk at the back of the church, so that softer instruments and voices can be heard among the louder drums and keyboards, etc.

passing notes A series of notes that help to link one chord to another— usually three or four notes on an ascending or descending scale.

pedal notes Notes (usually bass notes) which are held across a series of chords.

perfect pitch An inate ability to determine pitch. People with true perfect pitch can not only sing, say, the note of A♭ perfectly accurately at the drop of a hat, and give the name to any note played to them; they can also recognise when a note differs slightly from the normal tuning of 440 Hz. I heard of one lady who couldn't bear listening to one string quartet because they had tuned to something other than 440 Hz!

polyphony The number of notes that can be produced by an electronic keyboard at one time. Unlike, say, acoustic pianos or organs, where in theory all the notes of the keyboard can be played simultaneously, the technology of electronic keyboards is limited to 16, 32 or even sometimes 8 notes being played at one time. It is probably most noticeable when attempting a flourishing arpeggio all the way up the keyboard while holding down the sustain pedal; the first notes played will quickly begin to disappear as new notes are added.

push A term used in non-classical music where a beat appears to come earlier than it should. In fact, no beats are actually chopped; the emphasis is simply being brought forward from, say, the beginning of a bar, to a point half a beat or a whole beat earlier. When playing a push it is important to count steadily through the beats in your head so that none is chopped.

rall./rallentando   An Italian word meaning 'gradually slow down'. Usually marked at the end of a song.

related chords   A series of six chords that naturally fit together in any given key. It is surprising to see how many popular worship songs are made up entirely of these six related chords.

relative minor/major   Every major chord has a relative minor, and vice versa. The minor is worked out by counting down three semitones from the major, ie the relative minor of E major is C♯ minor; likewise, F minor's relative major is A♭ major. It can be effective to substitute a relative for the original to add interest to an arrangement, particularly since the relative minor/major is still likely to link in with the previous and following chord.

relative pitch   The ability to sing or recognise a given note by reference to another note already known. For example, I can identify the note of, say A♭ if I have already been given the note C; it is a process of mentally working out the interval from the note I know.

resolution   The point at which a note in a chord that seems to create a slight tension (if not an outright discord) moves to another note that 'resolves' the tension. For example, Csus⁴ to C: the F note moves to an E, and the tension is resolved.

rhodes   A word originating from a particular make of electronic keyboard, it has come to stand now for the sound that keyboard made—a warm, 'electric piano' sound, softer and more bell-like than a piano.

rhythm section   A collective term for the instruments providing the basic rhythm accompaniment—usually drums/percussion, bass guitar, keyboards, electric/acoustic guitars.

riff   A short musical idea or theme that occurs regularly through a song, adding interest and helping to create a memorable feel.

root note or tonic   The note after which a chord is named, eg C in C major, E in E minor, etc. It is the basic foundation of the chord.

root position   When a chord has the root note as the lowest of the three notes, the chord is said to be in root position. For example, the chord of D major in root position would have the note of D at the bottom, F♯ in the middle, and A at the top. See also **inversions**.

sampler   Often lumped together with synthesisers as 'electronic keyboards', the way they generate sound is in fact quite different. Samplers use the relatively recent computer technology found in today's compact discs to digitally record and replay 'real' sounds. Their advantage over synthesisers is that they can imitate real instruments far more effectively, although as instruments they are not so versatile.

SoF A shorthand reference to the *Songs of Fellowship* hardback songbook, in which the songs and hymns referred to can be found; throughout this book the song number is also given.

syncopation A term used to describe a series of notes or a rhythm that emphasises off-beats. Syncopation looks complicated on the stave, because of all the tied notes that written music demands—it should be heard and not seen to be appreciated.

synthesiser Any keyboard where sound is generated electronically rather than mechanically. Synthesisers generate simple sound waves that are manipulated to imitate a real instrument sound, or to create an entirely original sound.

tied notes A tie is a slightly curved line linking one note in a bar to another note, often in the next bar. It indicates that the note should be held for the combined length of the two notes, but only the first note should actually be played.

transposing Playing a piece of music in a different key from the one in which it was written.

triplet Three notes played in the space of two. Triplets take some practice to play accurately, as they do cut across the conventional rhythm of a song, but triplet rhythms within a melody are not uncommon, and usually don't present problems to a congregation to sing.

turn round The chord or chords used to link the end of a song or verse back to the beginning or on to the next verse. Alternatively, a turn round could be worked out to take you from the end of the song back to the chorus, or the last half of the song. If, when practising a song, you know that either the whole song, or just the chorus, is going to be repeated, it is a good idea to check that you have worked out a turn round.

velocity-sensitive Most synthesisers and electronic pianos these days are velocity-sensitive. This simply means that they behave like real pianos— the harder you hit the key, the louder the note produced. Velocity sensitivity is probably a prerequisite for everyone trained to play the piano, so check up that older or cheaper keyboards have this feature before you buy.

weighted keys A system on some electronic keyboards that makes the keys harder to press, thereby making the feel of the keyboard more piano-like. Pianists generally prefer this to conventional synthesisers, although the weighted action not only makes the keyboards more expensive, it also makes them heavier to carry.